T0078046

ARISE YE SLEEPING CHRISTIANS

Your Money is the Holy Grail

JAMES CAULFIELD

Order this book online at www.trafford.com
or email orders@trafford.com

Most Trafford titles are also available at major online book retailers.

Print information available on the last page.

ISBN: 978-1-6987-0979-6 (sc)
ISBN: 978-1-6987-0980-2 (e)

Library of Congress Control Number: 2021920793

Trafford rev. 10/08/2021

Trafford
PUBLISHING   www.trafford.com
North America & international
toll-free: 844-688-6899 (USA & Canada)
fax: 812 355 4082

Jesus said, "The first is, Love the Lord your God with all your heart and with all your soul and with all, your mind and with all your strength." The second is this: "Love your neighbour as yourself. There is no commandment greater than these."

To love yourself, you must preserve your mental health, nourish your body and do no harm to yourself. To love your neighbour you must do likewise.

Money is Jesus Christ's sacred elixir

Love is the fruit of prayer
Work is the fruit of love
Money is the fruit of work
Work performed for God is the fruit of Money
Salvation and Miracles are fruits
obtained by working for God
Your money is your Holy Grail
God's people use money to do God's work
Evil people use money to do Satan's work

CONTENTS

PROLOGUE

Stalin famously said of the Church, "The Pope! How many divisions, has he?" Less well known is Churchill's response that Stalin "might have mentioned a number of legions not always visible on parade".

The Catholic Church has more than 140,000 schools, 10,000 orphanages, 5,000 hospitals and some 16,000 other health clinics. Catholic aid agencies and their affiliates spend between £2 billion and £4 billion annually making it one of the biggest aid agencies in the world.

There is also a host of religious orders and other Catholic charities, most of the 200,000 Catholic parishes around the world operate their own small-scale charitable projects from education to health to social care. The Catholic Church is the largest and most significant non-state organisation on earth.

If the Church was not involved in the developing world, these services would not be provided at all. Research which has attempted to compare the performance of Catholic provision of education or health with that of other providers, Catholic institutions came out very well.

According to Kenneth White, of Virginia of Commonwealth University

"Catholic hospitals in the US are on average more efficient than equivalent secular hospitals and he found that Catholic hospitals, reach out to disadvantaged communities, providing more compassionate care and services than other providers".

Catholic-run, mission maternal hospitals in Africa are of the same or better quality than public facilities, and Church hospitals were also more likely to offer services to the poor.

Catholic social action goes beyond standard measures of performance. Indeed, Pope Francis has urged Catholic institutions always to put Christ front and centre, arguing that otherwise "we would end up a compassionate NGO" and "what would happen would, be like child-made sandcastles which fall down". Put another way, Catholic ethos and identity is crucial to the survival of Catholic social action and to the outstanding work of passing on the faith, in the face of a culture which is increasingly secular and hostile.

Aggressive secularisation is a threat to the full range of Catholic social action. Just last month Dame Louis Casey, the Government's integration tsar, asserted that "it was not okay" for Catholic schools to be against same-sex marriage., this exemplified the increasing pressure on Catholic institutions to conform to secular norms.

US President Barack Obama withdrew funds from Catholic projects to help victims of human trafficking because they would not commit themselves to providing abortions. The quality of the care being given to vulnerable women by the Church was not in dispute. It was seen as more important to ensure that all participating organisations were willing to agree to the ideological purity of the extreme pro-abortion position.

"A strategy more likely to yield long-term success for Catholic agencies is to follow the advice of Pope Francis, and Benedict XVI before him: to uphold our Catholic identify and ethos ever more boldly and to put into action the positive message of Church teaching on sexuality, life issues and the unique dignity and worth of all human beings. Church organisations should always insist on proclaiming the truth and sticking to a bold Catholic identity relying on the grace of God to transform lives in the most unexpected ways.

Life will not be comfortable facing the fact of reduced state funding. But secular opponents should also face the fact that if they insist on doing battle with the biggest charity in the world, they are putting at risk the wellbeing of millions of vulnerable and marginalised people. Catholic institutions must carry on delivering their services in the context of an ethos that has at its heart the dignity of every human life until natural death and the Church must continue to be the greatest force for good in the world today": *David Paton. Catholic Herald.*

The Church has a massive need of financial support to carry on and expand the Catholic drive to bring, spiritual and temporal works of mercy to the entire world. The Church has always been hampered by a lack of funds to achieve the goals set by Jesus Christ, because it has neglected to develop a coherent theology of money, thereby placing Christianity in a monetary Limbo, leaving the people to believe that they could use money without spiritual obligations. The Church has been content to gather the crumbs that fall from the Mason's financial table, when she should have recognised the sacredness of the people's work and the sacred power of the money they produce and harness it for the common good, instead of leaving it for non-Christians to abuse it and use it for evil purposes.

Jesus Christ was firstly a carpenter before He began His missionary career. His experience as a worker and His relationship with money is reflected in much of the His teaching.

His work was His father's will, the means of serving others, this is an attitude which all Christians should adopt. Christ's work ideal has suffered in the modern age because many workers have encountered the injustice of being forced to work solely for investor's profits, rather than doing the work of God.

Christian moralists have frequently attacked injustices in the work place, because of low pay rates, excessively long shifts and unhealthy atmospheres. Modern employment is often unchristian because of boredom and lack self-respect and without spiritual motives and incentives.

Christians should study the history of a secret culture that thrives on the power of money and the misuse of the money which working people create. Jesus Christ, the son of God was born and reared in a Jewish family. When, He revealed to His neighbours, the terms of the New Covenant as a holy relationship between God and humans, most of His neighbours were aghast and considered much of what He said as heretical but some followed Him and became Christians. The early Church was mainly comprised of Jews who believed Jesus was their Messiah and His New Covenant fulfilled them. Other Jews did not accept Him as their Messiah and continued live according to the precepts contained in the Old Testament, the resultant division continues to this day.

To all my brothers and sisters in all religious denominations and none, Jesus Christ unconditionally loves each and every one of you. He has no plan to destroy your religion or your laws. His only wish is to improve all that you have.

INTRODUCTION

Early man's relationship with his neighbour was surely expressed in terms of what one did to help the other. A traditional phrase "one good turn deserves another" is said when someone does something helpful or useful, in return for the person who has already done something good for one. An act of mutual cooperation is the basis of the barter system. To perform an act, one must do work of some kind. If person 'A' does day's work for person 'B', then person 'B' must later do a day's work for person 'A' to complete the barter. Work done, was the primary unit of the economy then and so it remains to this day, albeit in a different form.

At some stage in human development, it became necessary to record the number of work days done by the worker. In some primitive communities a Cowrie shell was given to a worker in payment for his or her work. The worker could exchange the Cowrie shell in exchange for food, useful items or services.

The Holy Grail; is money that is created by God's people through the work of their minds and hands and is thereby sacred. At least one tenth of discretionary income should be given to God to do His work. Money can do all things and cure all things. Money feeds the hungry, gives drink to the thirsty, clothes the naked, gives shelter to travellers, visits the sick, visits prisoners, and buries the dead. Money develops infrastructure for the common good.

Evil people can also use labour and God given raw-material to create money. Money in evil hands does the work of the Satan, Prince of darkness and has thereby become the greatest weapon on earth. It can destroy all things, kill all things, starve all things, corrupt all things and it is on course to wipe out all things.

Jesus Christ is the revolutionary who radically opposed and criticised Jewish practices and He drove the money changers out of the Temple. His Christian manifesto for a new universal religion of love and forgiveness became the basis of Western Civilisation. During His life on Earth He lived in the real world among real people, all of whom, He loved dearly.

Set against the ideals of Jesus Christ, our world at the beginning of the twenty-first century is not an ideal Christian place and multitudes are wondering, what has gone wrong? Why are so many people without love, without food, without housing, without education, without medical services, without human rights and so much more? Christian theologians have traditionally concentrated on spiritual aesthetics within the Gospels and the next life, more so, than Jesus Christ himself who frequently spoke of hands-on spirituality and temporal daily needs and wellbeing of people. Clerical thinking appears to be, if we get the theology right the rest will naturally fall into place and it has be recognized, that this approach has been successful to a large degree but the inherent shortcomings therein has however, allowed human living conditions to deteriorate on a global scale. Surely, it is time for Christians to analyse their understanding, and their practice of Christian values, and re-examine the Gospels for other possible interpretations that may be relevant to the basic needs of human beings. The widespread division among modern Christians is contrary to Jesus' wish that His followers should be united. Unity among Christians is possible if they work together to spiritualise Christian work practises and harness it for the common good and counter current laicized, subtle, concerted and insidious opposition to Jesus Christ.

Christian's have a basic obligation to familiarize themselves, with the teachings of Jesus Christ in order to understand what He is saying to them, e.g. "I did not come to destroy your (Canon) laws or your prophets (Hierarchy), I have come to fulfil". It is also essential for Christians to thoroughly acquaint themselves with the Gospels and search for overlooked instructions and eliminate false interpretations. It is also necessary to study the history of the Christian religion and to learn from the mistakes and false interpretations of some Christian leaders and to remember that most of what Jesus taught, was rejected by His Jewish neighbours, most of whom were scandalised and dismissed Him out of hand. Some Jews however, did accept His teaching and so began the Christian way of living.

In the pre-Christian era, the ancient Irish rejected the polytheism of the Celts and adopted monotheism instead, which conveniently prepared them for the coming of Jesus Christ. The pre-Christian Irish had developed a very enlightened constitution known as 'The Brehon Law', which enabled them to analyse the pros and cons of the Christian message when it was eventually brought to them, consequentially, it is said, that Ireland is the only country to be Christianized without bloodshed. The pre-Christian Irish had also adopted the circle as their spiritual symbol and they fused it with the cross of Christ, to preserve some precepts from their ancient constitution, which were in harmony with the Christian message. This Ancient Irish Cross aka; 'The Celtic Cross' became a symbol representing Jesus' assertion that He "did not come to destroy their Brehon law or their priests and holy men and women, but to fulfil their spiritual life", indicating that He did not object to their customs, but entreated them to consider another way of doing things and this should always be the philosophy of Christians, who deal with other sects.

"He came unto His own and His own received Him not". Most Jewish people do not accept that, a mere carpenter's son could fulfil them, preferring instead to adhere to their ancient belief, that a Messiah would be a powerful king-like figure and in the meantime they have clung to the morality of the Old Testament, dismissing the teaching of Jesus Christ. This gives them the freedom to pursue and justify any policy or programme that is important to them and is not in conflict with the tenets of the Old Testament, e.g. "An eye for an eye and tooth for a tooth". The troubled history of Judaism since the birth of Jesus is, largely due to fundamental moral differences, between Jews and Christians.

Scientists, who analyse an outbreak of a disease or a plague, scientifically search for the source of the problem and having identified the source, it becomes a matter of removing it. This study is an attempt to discover the source of widespread hunger and degradation in our world. It examines the extortion and abuse of monetary wealth and how such wealth is used to violate human rights and the tenets Christianity. President Dwight D. Eisenhower once said: "Every gun that is made, every warship launched, every rocket fired, signifies a theft from those who hunger and are not fed, those who are cold and have not clothes. The world in arms is not spending money alone. It's spending the sweat of its labourers, the genius of scientists and the hopes of its children". This is also a study of the historical connections between Judaism and Modern Freemasonry, since the formation of the Grand Lodge of England in 1717.

When the mysterious manifesto entitled: 'Protocols of the Elders of Zion' was published in Russia in 1903, it was met with pseudo outrage and condemnation by Freemasons and Zionists throughout the world. They described it as, anti-semitic, a hoax and a forgery. However, the unknown author was obviously well informed in the history of Zionist and Masonic involvement, in all the western revolutions of the 18th and 19th centuries. He or she, claimed to have had access to a secret manifesto of Zionists and Freemasons, to create a New World Order by instigating international turmoil, such as world wars, widespread violence, assassinations, massacres, the destruction of property, degradation of human rights and the financial enslavement of gentiles. If the 'Protocols' are figments of someone's imagination they have nevertheless, proved Protocols to be a very accurate prophesy of world affairs since that time.

Since the publication of the 'Protocols' in 1903 the world has witnessed, World War One 1914-1918, the barbaric and brutal Bolshevik Russian Revolution in 1917, the Spanish Civil War 1936-1939, World War Two 1939-1945, the Arab-Israeli war 1947-1948, the Korean War 1950-1953, the Vietnam War 1955-1975, the Suez Canal Crisis 1956, the Israeli-Arab six day war 1976, the Gulf War 1990, the Croation War 1991-1995, Afghanistan war 2001, Iraq War 2003, the Syrian Revolution 2011, the Libyan Civil War 2011, together with numerous wars in most of the African countries. The financial gossamer thread of Freemasonry and Zionist presence is visible in all these events.

Germany's economic success in the 1930s caused pandemic fear within the private banking community, because the German method proved, private financial service is in fact, the ultimate monetary scam. The Germans had demonstrated that their own financial system could bring them unlimited economic benefits without loans. If the German banking system became a worldwide phenomenon, it would break the financial shackles that enslaved Germany and much of the world. The Zionists and Freemasons embarked on a programme to defeat the Nazi financial system, and to reinstate Zionist/Masonic private banking in Germany.

In 20th century wars, at least 123 million people were killed and an unknown number were wounded, an inestimable destruction of property, equipment and infrastructure. It was entirely financed by naive working people throughout the world, who innocently trusted the banks and the financial institutions, who were secretly creaming off a portion of the worker's money and using it to invest in military hardware. If only, all that human energy and money had been used to develop better living conditions for the human race!

Zionists and Freemasons must be held responsible for a world of mayhem for the past three hundred years because they were in charge and giving the orders.

This study recognises that there is a very great number of God fearing, kind and compassionate people within Judaism who have been tarred with same brush that condemns the activities of militant Zionists, in the same manner that Catholics have been tarred, because Stalin, Mussolini, Hitler, King Henry VIII, and Spanish Inquisitors were associated with Catholicism.

122 years before the Protocols of the Elders of Zion were published in 1903, General Cornwallis' surrendering speech at Yorktown in 1781 prophesied future Masonic and Zionist activity: ***"Your churches will be used to teach the Jew's religion and in less than two hundred years the whole nation will be working for divine world government. That government that they believe to be divine will be the British Empire. All religions will be permeated with Judaism without even being noticed by the masses, and they will all be under the invisible all-seeing eye of the Grand Architect of Freemasons"***. He could have included: schools, colleges, universities, medicine, civil service, politics, military, government, state finance and much more.

Did the General have access to the plans, aspirations and goals of the Zionists and Freemasons at that time?

Was he a secret Freemason himself cooperating and facilitating the Brotherhood's great objective, to establish a Masonic State in America and eventually, a world government?

JEWS IN SPAIN AND ENGLAND

Jews occupied the Iberian Peninsula during the reign of King Solomon about 900 years before the arrival of the Phoenicians. Following the Babylonian King Nebuchadnezzar's conquest of Jerusalem and the destruction of the First Temple, Jews migrated en-mass to Iberia and established settlements throughout the territory where they lived and prospered in peace until about 489AD when they began to suffer persecution in the form of forced conversions to Catholicism.

During the period 653AD to 672AD the Converted Iberian Jews were stoned to death, burned alive or beheaded when they relapsed back into Judaism and in order to protect themselves the Jews developed the practice of pretending to be Catholics while secretly adhering to Judaism. They became Crypto Jews, i.e. 'Secret Jews.'

During the Spanish Inquisition many Jews converted to Catholicism. Forced baptism was contrary to the law of the Catholic Church, and theoretically, anybody who had been forcibly baptized could legally return to Judaism. Legal definitions of the time theoretically acknowledged that a forced baptism was not a valid sacrament, but confined this to cases where it was literally administered by physical force: a person who had consented to baptism under threat of death or serious injury was still regarded as a voluntary convert, and accordingly forbidden to revert to Judaism, however many of the converted felt it safer to remain in their new religion. From those a new social group appeared and were referred to as conversos or New Christians. Many conversos, now freed from the anti-Semitic restrictions imposed on Jewish employment, attained important positions in fifteenth-century Spain, including positions in the government and in the Church. This was the beginning of Jewish infiltration of Catholicism which enabled them to impose some of their religious beliefs on Catholics. Among many others, physicians Andrés Laguna and Francisco Lopez Villalobos (Ferdinand's court physician), writers Juan del Enzina, Juan de Mena, Diego de Valera and Alonso de Palencia and bankers Luis de Santangel and Gabriel Sanchez (who financed the voyage of Christopher Columbus) were all conversos. Conversos were now free to attain high positions in the ecclesiastical hierarchy and some became severe detractors of Judaism in order to maintain their cryptic masquerade. Some received noble titles and ranks and writers often expressed the opinion that most of the Spanish nobility descended from Jews and Freemasons.

The Cryptic practice of concealing Jewish identity has subsequently enabled them to penetrate and infiltrate any organisation they so wished.

Jews lived in England from 1066 when William the Conqueror brought a group of them from Rouen to England hoping for an injection of capital and commercial activity to offset his military spending. It was not an entirely pleasant beginning for Jews in England.

Christians of the middle ages were not allowed to charge interest when lending money because it was considered sinful to do so. However, the monarchs were happy to permit Jews to charge interest to finance wars and royal expenditure. The Jews were also happy as it brought them riches. In the following one hundred years the Jews had accumulated an estimated quarter of England's entire wealth, however, property obtained from usury passed to the monarch on the death of the usurer. The huge sum of fifteen thousand pounds sterling passed to King Henry II on the death of Aaron of Lincoln

The Knights Templar

About 1118AD, Hugues de Payens a French knight together with eight relatives and acquaintances founded a military order, called the Poor Knights of the Temple of King Solomon aka the Knights Templar. It is said that some of the founders were of Jewish extraction. Baldwin II, the king of Jerusalem, set up headquarters for them on the sacred Temple Mount and pledged to protect Christian visitors to the city. Religious leaders objected to the militarism of the order but in 1129 the knights received the formal endorsement of the Catholic Church and support from Bernard of Clairvaux, a prominent abbot and lavish donations and new recruits came pouring in from across Europe. The order could accrue wealth and land but the Templars themselves took vows of poverty. The knights adopted an austere code of conduct and a distinctive style of dress namely a red cross emblazoned on white habits. Their numbers grew in thousands and they established new chapters in all the European countries. They supported the Crusaders in battle and gained notoriety as fierce fighting men with a religious fervour and with a reluctance to retreat.

They established a network of banks that facilitated religious pilgrims to deposit money in their home countries and issued credit notes in order to withdraw money in Jerusalem. They accumulated vast quantities of money from their businesses together with generous donations and eventually became financiers to the Kings and other nobles in Europe. Some historians say they planned to create a Templar State on the island of Cyprus which they owned.

Pope Adrian IV (Nicholas Breakspear); 1100–1159) was elected Pope of Rome on the 4th December 1154 to his death in 1159. **Adrian IV** is both the only Englishman and the only inhabitant of the British Isles to have occupied the papal throne.

Pope Adrian IV, was so incensed with the practice within the Irish Church to give permission to people to dissolve their troubled marriages, that he actually gave the territory of Ireland to King Henry II of England on condition, that he bring the Irish Church into line with Roman regulations. English accounts mention a certain "Josce, Jew of Gloucester" as having financed the English expedition led by Strongbow in 1169 to conquer Ireland in defiance of a prohibition by King Henry II, who had forbidden the expedition and he later fined "Josce" 100 shillings for bankrolling the invasion which, established an unwelcomed English presence in Ireland and in the Irish Church, that has continued to this day.

Henry II's reign proved to be a benign period for Jews who lived on good terms with their Christian neighbours. They funded the construction of a large number of monasteries and abbeys throughout the England and Ireland, where they found refuge in times of persecution. However, clerics and Popes stirred up ill-feeling against them because they had crucified Christ and the Crusaders also considered Jews as legitimate targets. The heinous myth of 'the blood libel' was widely propagated throughout Europe. The myth suggested that William of Norwich and other Jews killed a young Christian boy and used his blood in the making of unleavened bread for the Passover.

Stephen Langton, the Archbishop of Canterbury introduced a directive which obliged Jews to wear a special badge for identification purposes. Many members of the ascendancy who were in debt to the Jews, organized mobs to ransack Jewish homes and business premises, in order to destroy loan records and to confiscate valuable property. English tolerance of the Jews ebbed and flowed with changes in the political climate until 1290, when King Edward I discovered an alternate source of finance in Italy among a group known as, the "Pope's usurers" and he then banished the Jews from England.

By this time the Knight Templars had become a powerful military organisation and they also controlled the financial and the commercial activities of most of the European countries. There is no doubt that Crypto Jews had secretly and successfully infiltrated the Templars creating the greatest financial institution in the world at that time. Some believe the Templars formed a pact with the Jews to further develop their banking businesses. The financial dominance of the Templars eventually brought about their demise, when European Monarchs began to worry about their loss of control over their own financial affairs. Following petitions to the Vatican from the heads of states, the Pope issued a Bull ordering the Templars to disband and many of the European states began to persecute and imprison the Templars. King Phillip of France was particularly ferocious in his efforts wipe out the Templars and he sentenced their Grandmaster, Jacques de Morley to be burned at the stake on the 18th March 1314. The execution of Jacques de Morley and the dispersion of the Knights Templars was calculated to reinstate financial independence of all the European countries but the Templars did not go away. They and their Jewish partners together with their money went underground and disappeared from sight. After a period of time they reappeared in a different form.

FREEMASONS

Freemason historians claim their society has been in existence for a very long time, how long is still a matter of scholarly debate. The craft of the stone mason began when early-man laid one stone on top of another and continued to lay more and more stones on top of each other until he had constructed the walls of a dwelling place. As time when on, his building skills developed enabling him to construct bigger and better buildings with stones and mortar. When bronze chisels became available he was able to carve stones into any shape he desired and the art of the stone mason began in earnest.

An examination of ancient stone built structures will reveal that, up to ninety per-cent of the walls were built with 'raw' field stones, this being the work of ordinary stone masons. The corners, arches, window and door openings are invariable executed in sculptured free-stone, this being the work of free-stone masons. It is believed that the title 'Freemason' evolved from the more highly skilled masons who executed the decorative work from free-stone such as marble, granite and sandstone which can be worked in any direction, because these stones have no grains. Their art work is visible in gargoyles, statues, wall plaques and lintels etc on ancient buildings.

The Freemasons formed a secret guild to protect and to maintain substantial remuneration for their special skills that were much sought after. Freemasons were the best paid workers in the building industry and they became very wealthy people. With the passage of time they acquired the skills of civil engineers and architects and were recognised as Master Builders. They were responsible for the construction of the great Catholic Cathedrals throughout Europe, England and Ireland. The first Great Cathedral was Arcibasilica di San Giovanni in Laterano, which was built on a site donated by Constantine the Great, as a gift to the Bishop of Rome in the fourth century.

Freemasons and Knight Templars

Over a long period of time Freemasons had established a good relationship with the Knights Templar, it was they who constructed Templar preceptories, churches, docks for shipping, harbour walls, road bridges and a multitude of other buildings. Following the Templars dissolution and subsequent persecution it was their Freemasonry friends who rescued them. The freemasons at that time were recognised public figures who openly plied their construction trade throughout England and Ireland. They were much admired for their expertise in construction and could freely circulate unmolested. They classed themselves as operatives in the building business. At this time the Freemasons and the Templars formed an indissoluble brotherly pact to work together in perpetual harmony to preserve each other's wealth and general wellbeing. It was agreed that henceforth their combined organisation would contain two distinct classes, namely 'Operative' (regular stone masons) and 'Accepted' (title for a voted-in member) for internal classification. The Templars could now openly pass themselves off as Freemasons while secretly running Templar business.

The Templars and the Freemasons were an exclusive Catholic organization until Henry VIIIs Reformation in 1532/1534. Following King Henry's dispute with the pope, he declared himself to be the supreme head of the church in England, encountering wide-spread opposition from Catholic England, to such an extent there was a possibility his plan might fail. He was obliged to surround himself with an assembly of like-minded cohorts, who were willing to do all that was necessary to establish a new independent Christian sect detached from the Vatican. It was a genocidal campaign to kill and enslave native English and Irish Catholics. King Henry's severe campaign martyred and cowed Catholics who refused to recognize him as their spiritual leader. The knowledge and the methods that Henry and his cohorts learned about controlling and abusing human beings at that time has been applied and enforced by the descendants of Henry VIII's evil cohorts in every nation that they conquered and controlled since that time i.e. native Americans, native

Australians, native New Zealanders, Native Asians. Now this group controls most of this hungry world

In order to guarantee and fulfil promised rewards to the members of this new assembly, Henry VIII created a new peerage awarding them land and privileges, not only for their own lifetime but for the lifetime of their descendants, forever. He further ordered all Roman Catholic churches, monasteries, abbeys, valuables and land be confiscated to finance the privileges which he granted to his supporters.

A Church of England priest recently complained that Protestant converts to Roman Catholicism were the cream of his church, whilst converts to Protestantism were the dregs of the Roman Catholic Church. Most of Henry VIII's supporters were the dregs of the Roman Catholic Church, (their descendants would later become members of Modern Freemasonry). They initiated a reign of terror against Catholics who opposed King Henry. Their methods to eliminate Catholic opposition included torture, execution, imprisonment, transportation, false evidence, enforced conversions, and much more, it successfully wiped out the Catholic working class but some Catholic members of the ascendency survived. They also introduced a series of new laws specifically designed to exclude Catholics from business, from economic activities, from education of any kind and from ownership of land, they calculated that if Catholics were kept sufficiently poor, they would either die out or emigrate, never to oppose the new regime in the future.

The Modern Freemasons adapted the old masonic constitution to reflect their new-found status and worked for the following one hundred and eighty- four years or so, to consolidate their wealth and privileges by strictly maintaining the tenets of their secret Fraternal Society, of modern freemasonry.

Oliver Cromwell

Oliver Cromwell's first teacher was an outspoken puritan by the name of Thomas Beard, who worked to purge the Church of England of its remaining Roman Catholic elements. Oliver Cromwell attended the predominantly puritan Sidney Sussex College and later Cambridge University. He also studied law in London, became deeply involved in the 'formation of the republicans' and he first entered parliament three years after Charles I came to the Throne. Over the following decade he developed a full-blown puritan and anti-monarchist philosophy. Cromwell was in Parliament in 1640 when the relationship between King Charles I and the Puritan-dominated 'House' collapsed and the civil war broke out two years later. Cromwell proved himself to be an excellent military leader and in 1644 he was promoted to Lieutenant General by Edward Montagu, Earl of Manchester. He was given the honour of leading the Parliamentary forces known as the "Roundheads" and earned the name 'ironsides' for himself and his regiment. On the 24th of June 1646 the Royalist capital, Oxford was captured by the Roundheads and Charles I surrendered and became a prisoner of Parliament.

> *"Many observers believe that Oliver Cromwell was a Freemason himself, and whilst no definite record still exists to prove this contention, it does seem extremely likely. Certainly his superior and close friend Sir Thomas Fairfax was a member of the Craft* (Freemasons), *and the Fairfax family in Ilkley, Yorkshire still have a* Masonic Temple"[1].

Cromwell's former chaplain, the Freemasonry Bishop of Chester, Dr John Wilkins, who married Cromwell's sister Robina, he was also a founder member of the 'Invisible College' now known as the 'Royal Society'. The Masons rightly calculated that a thorough knowledge of all the sciences would enable them to control and manipulate the masses. Studies of Cromwell's military and civilian administration have revealed that he did not destroy Masonic Temples and seldom confiscated Masonic property, *e.g.*, He spared the Rosslyn Masonic shrine in Scotland. Cromwell's puritan religion and republican philosophy dictated that Masonic philosophy and aspirations should coincide with his wishes and many suspect that Cromwell's blend of Freemasonry contributed to the formation of the Modern Society of Freemasonry and their subsequent relationship with the Protestant House

---

[1] The Hiram Key. apdx 1. C. Knight & R. Lomas.

of Handover. Some say that the Jews accepted Cromwell's invitation to return to England on condition that he execute King.

Following the execution of Charles I, a Dutch Jew, Menassed Ben Israel accepted Oliver Cromwell's invitation in 1656 and he and his people re-entered England. Cromwell was convinced that the Jews would develop commercial activity, from which he could raise taxes to restore the shattered national economy following the Civil War, and he was happy to re-admit them in spite of vigorous opposition from eminent judges, senior churchmen and merchants. The dubious relationship between Jew and Gentile which had blown hot and cold in medieval England, was again very much in evidence, and interested parties tried to re-expel them but the Jewish merchants proved their worth when they brought one and a half million pounds sterling to the commercial and financial fields, ensuring their acceptance where it mattered most.

King William of Orange

Francisco Lopes Suasso 1657 – 1710 was known within the Jewish community of Amsterdam as Abraham Israel Suasso. His parents were descendants of Converso families that left Spain after the Inquisition and eventually made their way to the Netherlands, where they were able to resume living openly as Jews.

Francisco was rich and politically astute, and it was to him that William of Orange approached for financial support in 1688, when he was preparing to invade England, to overthrow his father-in-law, the Catholic King James II.

Francisco provided the future William III of Britain with a loan of two million guilders, an astronomical sum at the time. But no less impressive is that when William asked him what he demanded in terms of collateral, Francisco responded – at least according to the legend – "If thou art victorious, I know thou wilt return them to me; art thou not victorious, I agree to having lost them."

William used the money to assemble a large army of 21,000 well-trained foreign soldiers which he brought to England in November 1688 on 500 ships together with additional troops and resources from Scandinavia and Germany. King James' depleted army was no match for William's well trained troops and he was forced to withdraw and William was installed as King of England.

By June 1689, King James II and the French were receiving reports that the English had turned against William and the Dutch and they began to plan a counter invasion of England from Ireland. On hearing of James' plan, William immediately sent his army to Ireland and defeated James at the Battle of the Boyne in July 1690 and decided the fate of Ireland and England. William had defeated the Jacobite

Army and King James' prospects of ever again regaining the Catholic Throne of England.

King William III defeat of Catholic King James II at the battle of the Boyne in 1690 establishing the supremacy of the Protestant religion and the Orange Order on these islands, which caused widespread discrimination against the Catholic people of Ireland and England.

In 1694 King William III, borrowed one million two hundred thousand pounds in gold at 8% from a group of privateers led by William Patterson and the King gave them a charter to issue notes to the public by way of credit to the same amount at a rate of 8% interest **i.e; Paterson's group could collect interest twice on the same money**. Therefore, the Patterson Group's reserves were calculated, £1.2M plus £96,000 annual interest of 8% on the loan to the King, plus the potential interest they could earn on loans of the same money to the public, and thereby created money out of nothing. This momentous scam was the embryo, from which the Bank of England hatched, effectively placing the finances of the English State in the private and secret hands of the Freemasons and Cryptic Jews, until the UK government bought 97% of its stock in 1946 leaving 3% with secret unidentified stock holders. Patterson's group installed King William III as head of the London Branch of Freemasons as a reward for granting them the 'charter'.

William Cobbett 1763-1835 said: *"I set to work to read the Act of Parliament by which the Bank of England was created in 1694. The inventors knew well what they were about. Their design was to mortgage by degrees the whole of the country, all the lands, all the houses, and all other property, and even all labour, to those who would lend their money to the State...the scheme, the crafty, the cunning, the deep scheme has produced what the world never saw before... starvation in the midst of plenty".*

William Cobbett's assessment of the money moguls grip on the people's wherewithal is more relevant today, as they have all but mortgaged all of mankind, in financial slavery, with invisible chains stronger than iron bands.

Before COVID 19, public debt had increased sharply in many countries, particularly during and after the Great Recession. Consequently, Global debt increased to a total amount of government debt exceeding $63.1 trillion, according to the Pew Research Centre's analysis of International Monetary Fund data.

In response to the COVID-19 crisis, the global debt-to-GDP ratio jumped by no less than 10 percentage points to 331% of GDP in the first few months of the pandemic alone. The total indebtedness of non-financial corporates had risen to $75 trillion at the end of 2019, twice its level in 2008

Worldwide, the private-sector debt made up about two-thirds of all non-financial-sector global debt in 2015.

Global debt hit a record high of over $250 trillion in the first half of 2020, led by a surge in borrowings in the U.S. and China.

JEWISH INSPIRED UNITED GRAND LODGE OF ENGLAND

Before the birth of Modern Freemasonry in 1717 when the Grand Lodge of England was established, an indispensable clause in the Freemason's constitution dictated that members had to be practicing Christians, this rule excluded Jews but they never-the-less became members, via 'the back door' using their traditional crypto practice, of superficially passed themselves off as Christians. Once inside Freemasonry they set about forming a new Masonic constitution that accepted new members who were simply, "Good men and true, who recognized a Supreme Being" this naturally included Jews. The Jews revealed to the Freemasons the awesome power of money and their methods of acquiring more and more wealth through their practice of charging usury on loans. Consequently, when Modern Freemasonry adopted Anderson's New Constitution in 1723, all "good men and true" could openly promote their financial businesses, this proved to be the perfect vehicle for Jews to ply their trade of usury which also appealed to the financially ambitious Masons. Jews and Freemasons had for a long time recognized an inherent commercial trait in each other and this relationship enabled them to jointly mould people into involuntary financial slaves. Jewish and Modern Masonic philosophies are alike; for all intents and purposes they are the same. The exclusion of women, the rejection of Jesus Christ, the practice of usury and democratic ideals became the agreed standard of Masons and Jews who together were motived by greed and a love for the 'power of money'.

Having infiltrated Modern Freemasonry the Jews took full advantage of their membership and they were soon dominating some of the Lodges and eventually created 'All Jewish Masonic Lodges' especially in America.

Pope Clement XII subsequently issued a Bull to warn Catholics of the dangers within Modern Freemasonry.

> *"Wherefore to each and all of the faithful of Christ we ordain stringently and in the virtue of holy obedience, that they shall not under any pretext enter, propagate or support the aforesaid societies known as Freemasons or otherwise named; that they shall not be enrolled in them, affiliated to them or take part in their proceedings; assist them or afford them in any way council, aid or favour, publicly or privately, directly or indirectly, by themselves or by others in any way whatever; under the pain of excommunication to be incurred by the very act without further declaration from us'.*[2]

The Antient (Ancient) Masons, who had remained faithful to their Roman Catholic roots, disapproved of

---

[2] 2 Pope Clement XII's Bull 'In Eminenti' 1738

the Protestant Freemason's association with Jews from the outset, disassociated themselves from the Protestant Masons and continued to operate according to their own traditional constitution but Protestant Freemasons continued to develop their own philosophies which included their commitment to place a Freemason on the English Throne.

> *"Freemasonry demands Liberty and Equality for the world; there shall be no kings, as well as no priests! All must be changed. The world has grown decrepit, cumbered as it is with the clumsy and ungainly structures which yet bear up the despotic ministers of Civil and Religious Despotism. These must be got rid of. All must be levelled down and filled up, that the great human family, freed from the trammels of religion and its irksome laws, may bask in the genial sunshine of liberty. Then comes Masonry with her mallet, to strike off the superfluities from the "rough ashlar" of humanity, her square and compass to regulate and measure its conduct, her two mystic pillars of strength and beauty, and all the tools for the building of the new temple of reform".* [3]

In Masonic philosophy there are no kings who rule by Divine right. Kings may be tolerated only when they subject themselves to a Masonic controlled parliament in which case, the Masons control the king.

---

[3]   Irish & English Freemasons M Di Gargano. Gill & Co

"The age of Enlightenment in the second half of the 18th century, with its growth of religious toleration and its general universal and liberal ideas, laid the foundations in western Europe and North America, for the emancipation of Jews and their participation as citizens in the life of the nations in the midst of which they lived, and whose members they became. The consequence was; less emphasis among the Jews on traditional religious attitudes, and more on assimilation of western secular culture. This movement (Zionism) emerged also in Germany, where Moses Mendelssohn (1729-86), a philosopher and friend of the great German writer Lessing, emphasized the spiritual and universal aspects of Judaism. He and a group of likeminded Jews, most of them residents of Berlin, and Konigsborg in Prussia, wished to win the Jews over to modern western civilization. The younger Jewish generation gladly seized the opportunity of intellectual enrichment and civic freedom, which the new movement, originally called by the Hebrew nae Haskalla (enlightenment), offered them. Many found their place in the new liberal and equalitarian societies emerging at that time in Europe and North America". [4]

The Freemasons had already penetrated the Church of England and many of their archbishops, bishops and

---

[4] Ency. Britannica 1973, p975, vol23.

ministers had been initiated into Freemasonry, therefore, no religious opposition was evident or expected from English Protestants. In 1723, the adoption of the Modern Freemason's constitution, initiated a rapid growth of Jewish Masonic alliances across the western world and their evident potential to weaken Christian values. The panic this caused in the Vatican at that time was later confirmed in 1859.

The Permanent Instruction of the Alta Vendita is a document, originally published in Italian in 1859, it was produced by the highest lodge of the Italian Carbonari and written by "Piccolo Tigre" ("Little Tiger"). Monsignor George F. Dillon believed this was a pseudonym of a Jewish Freemason.

The document details an alleged Masonic plan to infiltrate the Catholic Church and spread liberal ideas within it. The Carbonari had strong similarities to Freemasonry and so the document is seen by some as a Masonic document. In the 19th century, Pope Pius IX and Pope Leo XIII both asked for it to be published. It was first published by Jacques Crétineau-Joly in his book *L'Église romaine en face de la Révolution* in 1859. It was popularised in the English speaking world by Monsignor George F. Dillon in his book of 1885, the *War of Anti-Christ with the Church and Christian Civilization.*

It is still circulated by many traditionalist Catholics, who believe it accurately describes the changes in the church in the post-Vatican II era.

> **The Permanent Instruction of the Alta Vendita of 1859,** declared: *"Let the clergy march under your banner in the belief that they are marching under the banner of the Apostolic Keys. Lay your nets in the depths of the sacristies, seminaries, and convents. Let us spread vice broadcast among the multitude; let them breathe it in through their five senses; let them drink it in, and become saturated with it. Make men's hearts corrupt and vicious; and you will no longer have Catholics. Draw away the priests from the altars and from the practice of virtue. Strive to fill their minds and occupy their time with other matters. It is the corruption of the masses we have undertaken. The corruption of the people, through the clergy and the clergy by us. The corruption which, ought one day to enable us to lay the Church in the tomb".*[5]

King George III (1738-1820)

King George III's father Frederick Lewis, Prince of Wales (1707-1751) was first in line for the throne and he was also the first Royal Freemason. Frederick's self-indulgent and

---

[5] Alta Vendita published 1859

hedonistic lifestyle brought about his early death which placed his son George on the throne at the age of twenty in 1760. Soon after his coronation he married Princess Charlotte of Mecklenburh-Strelitz and over the next twenty-two years she bore him fifteen children. George III was well liked by his English subjects as he was English born he spoke English and preferred to live in England. In contrast to his father he was prudent, interested in agriculture and he was Tory. Georgian society declared his Court as dullest in Europe which contrasted sharply with the activities of his brothers who liked parties, drinking, gambling and running up huge debts. Three of George's brothers were initiated into Freemasonry. His brother Henry, Duke of Cumberland (1745-1790) became Grand Master of the Premier Grand Lodge of England. George III never entered Freemasonry himself, in fact he was opposed to the Craft, he said, "They were all felons and should be transported".

THE AMERICAN WAR
OF INDEPENDENCE

The institution of Masonry was brought to America from England early in the 18th century, possibly initially by Jews (Oppenheim 1910. 92). The Masonic society of secret rites had been formed to promote morality and fraternal accord among its members. Open to any male who vouched a belief in a Supreme Being. Freemasonry from the beginning eschewed any sectarian requirements. In Europe, where Jews had no legal rights of emancipation, Masonry offered a rare avenue to assimilation in the larger society. Acceptance of new members was by secret ballot, and Jewish candidates continued to receive the various degrees of the order.

In America, Masonry continued to provide a common ground for Jews and Christians. Among its members were the most influential business and political figures of the time, including George Washington, who was the Grand Master of Masons in Virginia. Jews served as Masters of individual lodges as well as Grand Masters of a number of states. In some communities, Masonry and Judaism were inseparably intertwined. When the Jewish community of Savannah, Georgia dedicated its new synagogue in 1820, the ceremony was conducted with Masonic rituals and trappings (Faber 1992. 115-16).

Many Jews who fought as patriots were Masons. Benjamin Seixas, Haym Salomon, Michael Gratz, Jonas Phillips, Mordecai Manuel, Noah and Solomon Bush are but a few historically recognisable Jewish Masons. The gravestone of Moses Seixas, a leader of Newport's Yeshu Israel, says. "He was Grand Master of the Grand Lodge of the Masonic Order of the State". American Jewish History. Norman H. Finkelstein

George III insisted on ruling the British Empire by Divine Right and refused to cooperate with the Freemasons and the Jewish Fraternity in America. He imposed trade taxes on the colonies which outraged the traders and the merchants, as the new taxes would swallow up much of their capital. The protests of colonists soon developed into a revolution that eventually established a new sovereign state, the American Republic, totally independent of England. Many historians have expressed doubts about the American War of Independence and suspect it was a **pseudo war** designed jointly by the Freemasons and Jews to establish a secular republic without encumbrances of Kings and Churches. Catholic values are antithetically feared by the Masonic-JewishFraternity and they created a constitution which intrinsically excluded any Christian function in state affairs. However, Jewish and Masonic religious values were not a problem. The imposition of George's new taxes was an opportunity for the Freemasons and the Jews, to galvanize the people to support a **just war** against an evil oppressor, a tactic to be used again and again in the future to justify Zionist-Masonic aggression, e.g. the sinking of the Lusitania, Pearle Harbour, the Bay of Tonkin, the Twin Towers, Iraqi weapons of mass destruction and Syrian chemical weapons, all enabled US politicians to convince Christian people to once again, send their precious sons and daughters to fight mythical enemies and that, their hard earned tax dollars should be spent making war.

The Continental Army 1775

President G. Washington's plan to recruit a Continental army in opposition to the British establishment infuriated King George III, who responded by reinforcing the British Military strength in the Colonies, and appointed highly qualified, experienced military generals and admirals to neutralize the Rebellion. The fact that the senior military men and virtually all the headquarter staff were Freemasons and G. Washington and his headquarter staff were also Freemasons, has caused many to speculate on the reluctance of Freemasons on both sides to kill their brothers on the other side! The nature of Freemasonry networking would suggest that the Freemasons on both sides knew in advance of the Masonic objective to create a New World Order and now they had an opportunity at last to begin, by creating a Masonic Republic in The Thirteen Colonies. This outrageous plan could not be publicised because of latent world-wide opposition to

Freemasons and Jews, would surely boil over and probably defeat them. In keeping with their practice to achieve their objectives covertly, the Freemasons and the Jews secretly decided that it was essential, that the War of Independence should proceed in order to convince the whole world, that a bunch of ordinary citizens were justly attempting to escape the oppression of a wicket King. Rank and file were coaxed to enlist in the continental army to secure **FREEDOM,** Freedom of religion, Freedom to vote in a democracy, Freedom to carry arms, Freedom of speech, Freedom in business, Freedom, Freedom ad infinitum. Ordinary people who in their former homelands had experienced oppression, discrimination, isolation, religious persecution, injustice etc.; fell for the scam, and enlisted in great numbers ready and eager to fight for an American Utopia.

Freemasons on the American side and brother Masons on the British side lined up their respective battalions of poor, gullible under educated rank and file and set them upon each other and then waited to see which side won, then ordered them to retreat and marched them to another location to engage the enemy again and the Masonic Jewish press kept the world informed about the progress of the war. Great emphasis was placed on the number of casualties, the loyal heroes, the loss of horses, conditions on the ground, the tactics of clever commanders etc., etc.; there was no end to the amount of suitable material to propagate the just cause of the Colonists and to convince the world that this was a real war and blood was flowing freely, however records show that the loss of Masonic and Jewish blood was mainly accidental.

Financing the American War of Independence

To maintain the charade, finance was needed to supply the Rebels with food, with military equipment, guns and ammunition, suitable clothes and footware, uniforms, horses, harness, carts, field-guns, etc.: Haym Salomon (aka Solomon) 1740-1785 was born of Jewish parents in Poland, he immigrated to American where he became a successful businessman dealing in political financial brokerage, he was to become an important financier in the American War of Independence. The American Superintendent of Finance, Robert Morris engaged him to convert French loans into liquid cash by selling exchange bills. This is how he and Morris financed Washington's Continental Army during the War of Independence against England.

Hayn Salomon being a member of the New York branch of the Sons of Liberty was arrested by the British in September 1776 as they suspected he was a spy. In traditional British style they pardoned him, on condition that he spend eighteen months on a British ship as interpreter for German mercenary soldiers serving with the British'. Salomon took advantage of his position to recruit the Germans into the American Army.

In 1778 Salomon was arrested again and sentenced to death. Again, he managed to escape, making his way with his family to the rebel capital in Philadelphia.[6]

Once resettled, Salomon resumed his activities as a broker. He became the agent to the French Consul as well as the paymaster for the French forces in North America. In 1781, he began working extensively with Robert Morris, the newly appointed Superintendent for Finance for the Thirteen Colonies.[7]

Records show that between1781-1784 Hayn Solomon raised $650,000 for George Washington's Continental Army and he was to become the quintessential American Hero when he somehow raised $20,000 at short notice to finance General Washington's final push to force the British surrender at Yorktown which was the last engagement between the Americans and the British in the American War of Independence

In August 1781, the Continental Army had trapped Lieutenant General C. Cornwallis in the Virginian coastal town of Yorktown. George Washington and the main army and Count de Rochambeau with his French army decided to march from the Hudson Highlands to

---

[6] "Haym Salomon". National Park Service, US Department of the Interior.

[7] Wiernik, Peter. "History of Jews in America". The Jewish Press Publishing Company, 1912. P.96.

Yorktown and deliver the final blow. But Washington's war chest was completely empty, as was that of Congress. Without food, uniforms and supplies, Washington's troops were close to mutiny.[8]

> Salomon negotiated the sale of a majority of the war aid from France and the Dutch Republic, selling bills of exchange to American merchants. Salomon also personally supported various members of the Continental Congress during their stay in Philadelphia, including James Madison and James Wilson. He requested below-market interest rates, and he never asked for repayment.[9]

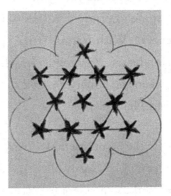

---

[8] "Haym Solomon: The Man Behind the Myth of the Dollar's Star of David". Retrieved. 29th June 2014.

[9] Wiernik, Peter. "History of Jews in America". The Jewish Press Publishing Company, 1912. P.95..

Haym Salomon is widely and well commemorated in the USA. However there is a legend, that during the design process of the Great Seal, President G. Washington asked what compensation Salomon wanted in return for his financial contributions to the American Revolutionary War. He replied that "he wanted nothing for himself but he wanted something for his people". As a result, the thirteen stars representing the colonies on the seal were arranged in the shape of the Jewish Star of David. This may be true as the Double Triangle is also be a Masonic symbol and its presence on the Great Seal is most likely a secret symbol of the Freemasonry-Jewish alliance, and allowing for the fact that so many Jews are Freemasons, it serves a dual purpose. The Israeli Star of David on the Great Seal of the United States' virtually confirms that Israel is a secret and the most favoured state within the USA. It has been said "The American State and the Israeli State are identical twins that were conceived and gestated in the same Masonic sac".

In 1893, a bill was presented before 52nd United States Congress ordering a gold medal be struck in recognition of Salomon's contribution to the United States.

In 1939, Warner Brothers released Sons of Liberty, a short film starring Claude Rains as Salomon.

In 1948 the USA recognized the Israeli State the same day it was proclaimed by the Jews.

In addition to Hayn Solomon many other Jewish merchants and bankers supported the Revolution with money and in kind. Joseph Simon from Lancaster Pa supplied the Continental Army at Valley Forge with famous Henry Rifles. Aaron Lopez bankrupted himself assisting the war. Abraham Levy and Phillip Russell stood their watch at Valley Forge and Jewish traders refitted their ships at great cost to enable them to counteract the aggression of the British Navy.

> *But how did the Jews save the American Revolution? As late as 1781 the war had not been won by the Americans nor was it lost by the British. Arms were being funnelled into the Colonies by arms merchants running the British blockade primarily from the tiny free trading Island of Dutch St. Eustatius. Jewish merchants and arms traders were a major presence on the island.*[10]

Historians speculate that the British had several chances for military victory in 1776–1777. If General Howe had advanced in December on the Continental troops quartered at Valley Forge, he might have readily overwhelmed them and possibly ended the war.

Howe submitted his resignation in October 1777; until it was accepted he spent his time in Philadelphia preparing

---

[10] Jewish Magazine; June 2004 edition.

his arguments for an expected parliamentary inquiry. Although he had twice as many men as Washington, the bitter memory of Bunker Hill made him highly reluctant to attack entrenched American forces. General Clinton replaced Howe as British commander-in-chief on May 24, 1778

In 1780 the population of England and Ireland was approximately 12.6 million while the population of the thirteen American colonies for that year was about 2.8 million including over 500,000 slaves, this gave Britain a 4.5:1 advantage. In fact, the British army had only the strength of a little more than the Americans because of British military commitments throughout the Commonwealth. The British mainly relied on impressment to fill their naval and army ranks whereas the American ranks were filled with volunteers willing to fight for independence.

In spite of the Americans determination to establish a republican state there was no guarantee that they would win the war. John E. Ferling says the odds were so long that the American victory was "Almost a Miracle."

Historians continue to debate whether the odds for American victory were long or short. On the other hand, Joseph Ellis says the odds favoured the Americans, and asks whether there ever was any realistic chance for the British to win. He argues that this opportunity came only once, in the summer of 1776 and the British failed that test. Admiral Howe and his brother General Howe had several opportunities to destroy the Continental Army among other reasons they blamed the weather. Ellis' point is that the strategic and tactical decisions of the Howes were fatally flawed because they overestimated the challenges posed by the Patriots. Ellis concludes that once the Howe brothers failed, the opportunity for a British victory "would never come again." The U.S. Army's official textbook argues that while the British difficulties were great, they were hardly insurmountable.

The American War of Independence is mysterious at every turn, yet the media has been propagating a version of events to give an impression, that everything about this conflict was a normal and necessary war. Looking back on the Revolution at the end of his life, John Adams wrote, **"The Revolution was affected before the War commenced. The Revolution was in the minds and hearts of the people."** Some believe the American Revolution was certainly in the minds of Jews and Freemasons who had a long term plan to establish a Republic based on their own libertarian philosophy which would include a democratic system where the people vote for leaders rather than suffering beneath the power of a monarch.

The leaders of the revolution propagated a manifesto which emphasised a long list of injustices imposed by King George III on ordinary people and promised a long list of freedoms. Most of the colonists had only a superficial knowledge of political philosophy and did not have time acquaint themselves with the sophisticated Enlightenment treatises on political philosophy or on the rights of man they only understood what they saw on a day to day basis and followed their instincts regarding their liberty. They knew and understood what the British Empire was planning for their future regarding the imposition of additional taxes and they were not willing to submit to a foreign opinion of who had the right to tax them. Negotiations across the Atlantic moved the British Parliament to agree to most of the American demands short of independence but the Masons and their Jewish friends could see the 'promised land' and joyfully crossed the 'Rubicon', there was no turning back.

It was 'AMEXIT' so to speak, the majority of American people and Congress were united in their determination to secure independence from the Mother England and George III. Thomas Jefferson's view of a government of the people within a monarchy was, the Kings would be "the servants and not the proprietors of the people". This suggested the King would be subject to the people in a democratic state.

Benjamin Franklin expressed an opinion that a government was really the same as a business where the directors were employees of the company shareholders (the people of the state). The members of the parliament were the servants of the people and were instructed by the people through the voting system. This radical concept would undermine the traditional natural order of a monarchy, where the monarch was believed to be ordained by God. When this notion of radical election of governments grew in the minds of the people it became clear that the electors could dispose of a government that failed to comply with the will of the people. This conceived "a government of the people, for the people and for the people", as described by Abraham Lincoln in his time. Once the people rejected the sacred rite of Monarchs to rule them, they could in good conscious accept a secular government that was strictly separated from the Church.

In 1789 it was proposed to amend the US constitution as follows: *"Congress shall make no law respecting an establishment of religion, or prohibiting the free exercise thereof..."*. However this amendment was worthless as far as Catholics were concerned, they have suffered all kinds of discrimination in the USA because of their religion.

THE PSEUDO WAR OF
INDEPENDENCE

There exists a large body of evidence showing that the American War of Independence was planned for the sole purpose of creating a Jewish-Masonic state. The Jewish-Masonic global organisation had set their sights on the English Colonies in America as the best place to establish their own longed for state, which would incorporate Jewish philosophy of the Old Testament, secular ideals and aspirations, free of the influence and the teaching of Jesus Christ, Popes and the religion of Monarchs. In order to trick the colonists into supporting them, covert publications explaining the need for independence to free them of the cruel and greedy King George III, was widely broadcast to incite the people. European and American Jewish-Masons had secretly and treasonably agreed to initiate a revolt in order to achieve independence from England. The fact that most of the leaders in America and most of the British Military leaders were Masons required careful military planning to insure they did not kill brother Masons. Historical records of military engagements have revealed that commanders on both sides had opportunities to press forward and eliminate their opponents, but they declined to do so for dubious reasons. Between 1775 and 1783 (8years) 8524 colonists and loyalists were killed in the battle for independence. In the Civil War of 1861 to 1865, (4years) a total of 204,070 US &

CS were killed in battle. The casualties of the Revolution, a little over one thousand per year seems to suggest it was not an all-out war. It was more like a huge movie set, where the various engagements were carefully choreographed but accident prone, leaving genuine dead soldiers for the press to record and describe images of war, for home and empire consumption, in order to convince all and sundry interested parties, that there was a real war in progress.

The final scene was played out in Yorktown where the British villain, Gen. C. Cornwallis commanded a hungry and disillusioned army, defeated by an assembly of gun-happy civilians, surrounded on land and by sea, with no option but to raise the white flag and symbolically hand over his sword to the victors. He availed of the opportunity to prophesize the fate of the Christian religion, gleaned no doubt from his knowledge of the Zionist-Masonic long term programme to dominate the whole world.

> *"Your churches will be used to teach the Jew's religion and in less than two hundred years the whole nation will be working for divine world government. That government that they believe to be divine will be the British Empire. All religions will be permeated with Judaism without even being noticed by the masses, and they will all be under the invisible all-seeing eye of the Grand Architect of Freemasons*[11]

---

[11] General Charles Cornwallis. Yorktown

When this 'Villain' had thus delivered his final lines the USA was born. Truly this was the stuff of the futuristic Hollywood where Jews and Freemasons reign supreme. General Cornwallis' speech however, reveals that he was fully aware of the methods, practises and aspirations of Jews and Freemasons and the traditional secret activities of 'crypto' Jews and 'crypto' masons who adopt secret public images of, Bible Thumping Christians, fundamental Koran loving Islamists, radical ISIS guerrillas or red hot Communists, while remaining fundamental Jews and Freemasons.

THE CATHOLIC KNIGHT's blog: "I always get a chuckle when I hear Evangelicals tell me that the United States of America was founded as a "Christian nation." No, I tell them, that's what it was before the American Revolution, when the colonies were ruled by a Protestant Christian king. After the Revolution, the colonies ceased to be Christian, and became the world's first Masonic nation! Granted, America's founding fathers were cooperative with Christians, mainly because they had to be, but don't think for one second that those same founding fathers had any intention of America keeping any trace of a Christian form of government. The founding fathers agreed that the moral foundations of religion were useful in building the country, but they kept it strictly to **amoral** understanding of the Christian religion, as all good Masons do. The idea of American government actually recognizing the real authority of any particular Church was repugnant to them. Of course, most repugnant to them was the Catholic Church, which the founding fathers were determined to keep in its place. Need I remind my readers that following the American Revolution, Catholics suffered some of their greatest indignities at the hands of those who claimed the highest loyalty to the U.S. Constitution and the American Revolution?

Freemasons don't rule America in the literal sense, like a king might rule his subjects, but they do rule America in principle. In fact, the United States was founded on Freemasonry, and thus it is the world's first Masonic Nation. The idea being that Freemasons rule America through its system of government designed and ordered through Masonic principles. The idea of democratic republicanism (popularly and incorrectly referred to simply as "democracy") is Masonic in origin, a product of the Enlightenment era, which opposes Christian monarchy, the foundation of western civilization.

I want to make this very clear. Western civilization was founded on Christian monarchy. Kings and queens were subject to the ecclesiastical authority of the Catholic Church, which had both the power to coronate them and excommunicate them. By coronating them, the Church gave them power. By excommunicating them, the Church diminished their power, and sometimes dethroned them entirely. Thus western civilization was ruled by a Christian system of government during the middle ages. It was only after the Protestant Reformation that we start to see significant problems with these monarchies, which in due course gave birth to the Enlightenment and the rise of Modern Freemasons. The Modern Freemasons in turn toppled the monarchies, or at the very least diminished their authority, thus giving us democratic republicanism.

The problem with democratic republicanism, besides it being an unchristian form of government derived from ancient Pagan principles, is that it always leads to socialism. This can be seen in developments within various democracies throughout the world, and even here in the United States, which continually slides deeper into socialist rule.

Many Catholic Americans don't understand the intrinsically anti-Catholic nature of Freemasonry. You have to understand that in America, Freemasonry has already accomplished most of its goals. The government is totally Freemason. The democratic road to socialism is well underway, and nothing less than a total collapse of Washington DC can change this. Therefore, there is no need for Freemasons to work so hard in the United States. Most of their work is already finished. The primary function of most American Freemasons is now mainly fundraising, to help spread Masonic ideas around the world. In Europe Freemasonry takes on a much more openly anti-Catholic role, as it continually tries to undermine the influence of the Catholic Church there.

Posted by Catholic Knight at Monday, October 2009

Evidence of Masonic and Zionist infiltration of the Catholic Church has been mounting in recent years. They have indeed gained access to Catholic seminaries where they propagate their own blends of liberal theology encouraging spiritual permissiveness which cause students to question the teachings of Jesus Christ. e.g., the phrase 'life begins at conception' is a false statement, because conception can only take place when existing life in sperm and ovum are joined together. Conception is a stage in the life cycle rather than its beginning. However, permissive theorists use the phrase 'life begins at conception' to explain, that consentual sex is harmless and sinless fun when conception cannot take place, such as: nocturnal emissions, masturbation, LGBTQIA activities etc. This immoral philosophy was classed as fornication by Jesus Christ when He banned it but some of His followers have succumbed, to base sexual temptation implied in this philosophy, because they felt, they were sexually constrained by rigorous religious conventions. Widespread sexual abuse by some of the clergy within the Catholic Church has been extremely detrimental to Catholicism. Such abuse surely emanated from this false philosophy, which Jesus Christ's enemies deliberately planted in Catholic seminaries, in order to destroy Catholicism from within.

FREEMASONS IN
WESTERN MILITARY

It is important to investigate the presence of Freemasons within western militaries since the beginning of the eighteenth century because politicians depended on them to enforce their policies. There are large volumes of the historic military involvement in all the social and economic changes that have taken place throughout the world. Freemasons in the US military are relatively well known but less so regarding the British Commonwealth.

Modern Freemasonry was organized in England early in the 18th century and its traditional roots are to be found there. The American Masons were leaders in the War of Independence and Masons in the British Army opposed them. Many well-known British Freemasons involved in the French and Indian War and the American Revolution. James Wolfe (1727-1759), a prominent British commander was killed while capturing Quebec from the French in 1759, he was a member of a British military lodge in Minden, Germany. Lord Sir Peter Parker (1721-1811) led the failed British expedition against Charleston in 1776, he later promoted and became the ranking officer in the Royal Navy (Admiral of the White). He served as Grand Master of the Grand Lodge of England (Moderns) from 1787-1811. Sir George Rodney, who commanded the

British fleet that defeated the French in the Caribbean in 1782, was a Freemason. Lord Charles Cornwallis, commanded the British Army in the southern colonies in the final phase of the American Revolution, he was given the privilege of delivering the Masonic funeral oration for the American General, Baron DeKalb, who was killed at the Battle of Camden in 1780. There is no evidence to confirm that Cornwallis was a Freemason but many members of his family were affiliated with Irish lodges, one of them served as Grand Master of Ireland. Some famous Americans of that era have been listed as Masons but there is no absolute evidence to confirm their membership. It is also difficult to definitely ascertain who in the British ranks were affiliated to the Masons. Lord George Sackville 1716-1785, served in European wars against the French in the 1750s, and later commanded British military forces in North America during the Revolution. He was a Freemason, and was the Grand Master of the Grand Lodge of Ireland in 1751. Generals William and Clinton Howe were commanders of British regiments that were charted by the Grand Lodges of Scotland and Ireland in North America during the French and Indian War. (not to be confused with the Howe brothers, Richard and William).

Lord Richard Howe ("Black Dick") was the commander the British Navy during the Revolution, and his brother Sir William, commanded the British Army in North America from 1776-1779. Both of them were very sympathetic to the American cause and only agreed to take assignments in America as peace commissioners Sir William covertly corresponded with Benjamin Franklin and by extension with George Washington throughout the war. This correspondence would suggest that there was a secret Masonic plan to establish a Masonic state in America and forms one of the many mysteries of the war. Howe's American War letters were burned by his descendants in the 19th century causing some to suspect that they contained evidence of treasonous activities.

British Masons were very much in evidence during the Napoleonic Wars. Sir John Napier (1782-1853) served as a Lt General in the British Army in Portugal in 1810. He later served in the War of 1812 against the US. He was made a Master Mason in a British military lodge in Germany in 1807. Sir John Moore (1761-1809), the commander of British forces in the Iberian Peninsula, became a Mason in Halifax, Nova Scotia in 1781. Moore was killed in action against the French in 1809, and was succeeded by Arthur Wellesley, Duke of Wellington, who was born in Dublin on the 1st of May 1769 and became the most famous British military man of the 19th century. Wellington was a member of his family lodge in Trim, Ireland, and his brother later served as Grand Master of Ireland. His prominent place in military history was assured following his defeat of Napoleon (probably a Mason) at Waterloo in 1815, with the assistance of the Prussian Army, commanded by Field Marshall Bluecher, who was also a Mason. There are no conclusive records to establish whether or not the great British Admiral of Trafalgar Viscount Horatio Nelson (1758-1805), victor of Trafalgar was a Mason, however there are a number of Masonic references to him and his funeral service was conducted by a Masonic lodge in Portsmouth.

Sir Garnet J. Wolseley (1833-1913) became a Mason in 1854 in travelling lodge No 728 under the Grand Lodge of Ireland and he served as its Grand Master in 1893. Wolseley served in the Crimean War where he lost an eye and later served during the Sepoy Mutiny in India and he commanded British forces in Asia and African colonial wars in the 19th century.

General Frederick S. Roberts (1832-1914) better known as "General Bobs", Earl of Kandahar, Pretoria, and Waterford (Ireland). Roberts', first command was in India and he saw action in the Sepoy Mutiny and the siege of Delhi where he was awarded the Victoria Cross. He was involved in the relief of Lucknow and the Battle of Cawnpore. He also saw action the second afghan war in 1882, and was made the Earl of Kandahar as a result. In 1900 during the Boer War in South Africa, he led British forces to break the siege of Kimberly.

Lord Horatio Herbert Kitchener was born in County Kerry, Ireland 1850 – 1916. For his service in the British Army in India he was given the title,' Earl of Khartoum'. He re-conquered the Sudan for Britain in 1898, defeating the

Sudanese at Omdurman and Khartoum. He was promoted to Commander in Chief in India from 1902-1909, and was later promoted as Commander in Chief of the British Army. Kitchener was given the task of enlarging the British Army from 6 to 62 divisions after the outbreak of World War One, and under his dedicated leadership he successfully managed to enlist about one million recruits to make up 62 divisions many of these men were sacrificed in the defeat of Germany. He used his own picture on posters which read "Your Country Needs You" in his recruiting campaign. The American military later used a modified copy of his poster in the image of Uncle Sam to recruit in the USA.

Kitchener became a Mason in a lodge in Egypt, and in 1885 was one of the founding members of Drury Lane Lodge #2 127 in London. He was named a Past Grand Warden of the Grand Lodge of England in 1897, and served as the District Grand Master for the Sudan in 1899. Kitchener was drowned in 1916 when the cruiser (HMS Hampshire) on which he was traveling to Russia, struck a mine and sank. Another notable British Mason served during World War I he was Marshal Sir John French (1852-1925), 1st Earl of Ypres, commanded the British Expeditionary Force which landed in France in 1914. In 1884 French served in the Nile Campaign of under Wolseley, and with the British cavalry in the Boer War (1899-1901). He served as Chief of the Imperial General Staff from 1912-1914. French became a member of Jubilee Masters Lodge #27 12 in London in 1906.

Other prominent Masons in the British Army included: Field Marshal Sir Douglas Haig (1861- 1928). Haig had an unusual Masonic career, being initiated in Elgin Lodge #91 in Leven, Scotland in 1881, but not becoming a Master Mason until 1924. Sir John Jellicoe (1859-1935), the Commander of the Grand Fleet and the victor at Battle of Jutland, did not become a Mason until he was 63 and serving as the Governor General of New Zealand, a position he held from 1920-1924. He served as Grand Master of the Grand Lodge of New Zealand from 1922 to 1924. Sir Harold R. L. G. Alexander, Viscount of Tunis, was also a Mason. He was a member of Athlumney Lodge #3245 in London and served as its Master in 1938 and 1939. He was a Royal Arch Mason serving as a Grand Steward and Grand Warden of the Grand Lodge of England. Winston Churchill, British Prime Minister and Lord of Admiralty during World War Two, was also a Freemason. The records of British Military Masons in World War II include the Commander in Chief HRH, King George VI (1895- 1952). The King was a fervent Mason from the time of his initiation in 1919 into Naval Lodge #2612. In 1922 he became Grand Senior Warden, and in 1924 Provincial Grand Master of Middlesex. He awarded the rank of Past Grand Master on his ascent to the throne in 1936. He was also affiliated with Glamnis Lodge in Scotland, and later he was installed Grand Master Mason of Scotland

THE FRENCH REVOLUTION 1789

The French Revolution of 1789 was the most startling event in the history of Europe since the fall of the Roman Empire. A radical new phenomenon appeared in France which astounded the civilized world. An unknown group of uneducated lower class people had apparently organized a successful revolution against all other classes in the state, voicing high sounding radical and unheard of slogans while promoting and advocating horrific solutions to advance the betterment of the people. They successfully conquered all of France and destroyed every feature of civilized living and national tradition, from Monarch, church and clergy, upper class citizens, constitution, flag, calendar, and place names, to coinage. Analysis of the French revolution reveals it was not the work of Frenchmen to improve living conditions of the people it was rather a foreign plan to employ scorched earth methods to utterly destroy France and all that it stood for, their battle cry was, **"overturn the throne and the altar"**. This was the conclusion of Robes Pierre and Sir Walter Scott and it is evident that Jews who held high places in the Revolutionary Councils were involved.

Did the French emancipate Jews or did French Jews emancipate themselves?

In any event they gained a foothold in politics for the first time since the fall of Jerusalem in 70 A.D: The granting of emancipation to the Jews was not an easy matter, there were many objectors. Count Stanislaw de Clermont-Tonnerre proposed to grant them full rights of citizenship according to the most general principles. Religion was a private affair. The law of the state need not and ought not, impinge upon it. Clermont-Tonnerre was promptly contradicted on this last vital point by the Abbé Maury. The term 'Jew', said the Abbé, did not denote a religious sect, but a nation, one which had laws which it had always followed and by which it wished to continue to abide. 'To proclaim the Jews citizens would be as if to say that without letters of naturalization and without ceasing to be English or Danish, Englishmen and Danes could become Frenchmen.' But Maury's chief argument was of a moral and social order. The Jews were inherently undesirable, socially as well as economically. They had been chased out of France, and then recalled, no less than seven times – chased out by avarice, as Voltaire had rightly put it and readmitted by avarice once more, but in foolishness as well. The Jews were already holding 12 million mortgages in Alsace alone, he informed his colleagues. Within a month of their being granted citizenship they would own half the province outright. In ten years they would have conquered all of it, reducing it to nothing more than a Jewish colony – upon which the hatred the people of Alsace already bore the Jews would explode.

At that time there were 39,000 Jews living Alsace and Lorrraine which had become part of France under the terms of the Westphalia in 1648. In the 18th century a small number of Jews had taken advantage of the British Government's Illuminati non-ideological approach and the French had noticed the advantages England had achieved in doing business with the Jews. "Let us restore them to happiness, to homeland and to virtue by restoring them to the dignity of men and citizens; let us reflect that it can never be politic, whatever anyone might say, to condemn a multitude of men who live among us to degradation and oppression". Thus spoke the man who was soon to lead the most degrading and oppressive regime in European history to that date. Indeed, it is striking how those who spoke most fervently for the Jews – apart from leaders of the Jewish community such as the banker Cerfbeer and Isaac Beer – were Freemasons or Illuminati.

Thus in the two years before the crucial debate on September 27, 1791, writes General Nechvolodov, "fourteen attempts were made to give the Jews civic equality and thirty-five major speeches were given by several orators, among them Mirabeau, Robespierre, Abbé Grégoire, Abbé Siéyes, Camille, Desmoulins, Vernier, Barnave, Lameth, Duport and others.

"Now there is a singular comparison to be made", says Abbé Lemann, "all the names which we have just cited and which figure in the Moniteur as having voted for the Jews are also found on the list of Freemasons, is this coincidence not proof of the order given, in the lodges of Paris, to work in favour of Jewish emancipation?" The emancipation of the Jews in 1789-1791 was carried out chiefly by the Freemasons many of whom were Jews. This seems to confirm that Jewish psychology coincides with central Masonic rituals and rites. Judaism and Freemasonry were already inter-dependent and inter-related in England since the beginning of the 18th century.

The first stage of the Revolution, from 1789 to 1791 was dominated by the Masons, whose numbers had grown at an astonishing rate in the pre-revolutionary years. Adam Zamoyski writes that "there were 104 lodges in France in 1772, 198 by 1776, and a staggering 629 by 1789. The membership included virtually every grandee, writer, artist, lawyer, soldier or other professional in the country, as well as notable foreigners, such as Franklin and Jefferson – some 30,000 people" 11.

According to Doyle "Between 800 and 900 Masonic lodges, were founded in France between 1732 and 1793, two-thirds of them after 1760. Between 1773 and 1779 well over 20,000 members were recruited. Few towns of any consequence were without one or more lodges by the 1780s and despite several papal condemnations of a deistic cult that had originated in Protestant England, the élite of society flocked to join. Voltaire was drafted in on his last visit to Paris, and it was before the assembled brethren of the Nine Sisters Lodge that he exchanged symbolic embraces with Franklin."

In 1791 a split began to emerge between the more moderate liberal Masons, the great majority, who had been responsible for liberal reforms like the Declaration of the Rights of Man, and a more violent and revolutionary minority. The split was reflected in the composition of the Convention elected in 1792. It was divided between 'Montagnards' (Jacobins) on the left, led by Marat, Danto, Robespierre and the Parisian delegates and the'Girondins' on the right, led by Brissot, Vergniaud and the 'faction of the Gironde'. The Montagnards were identified with the interests of the Paris mob and the most radical ideas of the Revolution, the Girondins – with the interests of the provinces and the original liberal ideals of 1789. The Montagnards stood for disposing of the king as soon as possible; the Girondins wanted a referendum of the whole people to decide.

Napoleon Bonaparte came to power in a bloodless coup d'état on the 9th of November 1799. He inherited a Revolutionary France that had stagnated into corruption, poverty and violent settling of old scores. His political leadership brought peace and tranquillity for a period. There is no conclusive proof that Napoleon was a

Freemason, but many of his military officers, most of the Marshals and members of the Grand Council of the Empire were. Four of his brothers were Freemasons and Empress Josephine was a member of a female lodge. Napoleon did adopt the title 'Protector Freemasonry' when he became emperor in 1804. As First Consul, Napoleon was more Powerful, than Louis XIV because he controlled the armed forces of a military state which was devoid of civil, legal, religious and other institutions which were neutralised during the Revolution. He was free to imprint on a blank national canvas everything he personally considered appropriate for the people of France. He established by plebiscite, a pseudo monarchy democratically based on the Revolution. Napoleon hastily crowned himself Emperor before the pope could complete the crowning ceremony. He conquered most of Europe imposing his vision of monarchism on the kingdoms and Grand Duchies of Italy, Venice, Rome, Naples, Lucca, Dubrovnik, Holland, Mainz, Bavaria, Wurttemburg, Saxony, Baden, Hesse-Darmstadt, Westphalia and Spain, giving them greater monarchical power and they were all ruled by Napoleon's extended family. He planned to make Europe one vast monarchy over-ruled by Paris saying **"The French Empire shall become the metropolitan of all other Sovereignties"**. He saw himself as the pillar of royalty in Europe.

The French Revolution had given the Jews their first political victory and Napoleon personally gave them their second. The Paris Moniteur reported from Constantinople on the 22nd of May 1799 that Napoleon had published a proclamation inviting the Jews of Asia and Africa to submit to his flag in order to re-establish ancient Jerusalem. He had already supplied a large quantity of arms for their battalions threatening Aleppo. Napoleon convened an assembly of Jewish Notables to supply clear unambiguous answers regarding Jewish practices: Did the Jews regard Frenchmen as brothers, did they regard themselves as native citizens of France and obey her laws without exception, do Judaic law distinguish between Jewish and Christian debtors, do Jews permit mixed marriages? Some Jews rejected Napoleon's proclamation while other Jews received the news with unbounded joy. Abbé Lemann said "They grovelled in front of him and were ready to recognise him as their Messiah". A Sanhedrin of 46 rabbis and 25 laymen from all parts of Western Europe assembled in Paris in February and March 1807 and began with the words "Blessed forever is the Lord, the God of Israel, Who has placed on the throne of France and of the kingdom of Italy a prince according to His heart. God has seen the humiliation of the descendants of ancient Jacob and He has chosen Napoleon the Great to be the instrument of His mercy". They assembled under his powerful protection in the good town of Paris, to the number of seventy-one doctors of the law and notables of Israel, we constitute a Great Sanhedrin, so as to find among them a means and the power to create religious ordinances in conformity with the principles of their holy laws, and which would serve as a rule and example to all Israelites. These new ordinances were intended to teach the nations that our dogmas are consistent with the civil laws under which the Jews could live, in unity with all from the society of men.

Napoleon's prestige among the Jews reached new heights when he succeeded in breaking up the feudal castes of Mid-Europe by introducing the equality of the French Revolution, he achieved more for Jewish emancipation than had been accomplished in the preceding three centuries. As part of recognising the Jewish community, he established a national Israelite Consistory in France, with sub-organisations for various regions. It was intended to serve as a centralising authority for Jewish religious and community life. Similarly he established a 'Royal Westphalian Consistory of the Israelites'. This served as a model for other German states until after the fall of Napoleon. German Jews have historically regarded Napoleon as the major forerunner of Jewish emancipation in Germany. When the government required Jews to select surnames according to the mainstream model, some are said to have taken the name of Schontheil, a translation of Bonaparte. In the Jewish ghettos legends grew up about Napoleon's actions and Italian Jews often chose Napoleon and Bonaparte as their given name in honour of their historic liberator.

An unknown artist painted a picture (see front cover and appendix 2) of a Jewish mother posing Madonna-like dressed in the national colours of France she is cradling an infant baring a strong resemblance of Napoleon, the Jewish Messiah. Ironically and mysteriously N.M. Rothchild and Sons bank in London funded Wellington and the consequential annihilation of the French Messiah at Waterloo confirms that Jewish financial institutions have the necessary resources to finance wars, which enables them to make huge profits in 'tearing down and building up'. Wellington was born in Dublin on the 1st May 1769. An obelisk in his honour, 62m in height stands in Dublin's Phoenix Park, it is the tallest obelisk in Europe. More than 30% of his army at the Battle of Waterloo were Irish soldiers. Many believe that his Catholic Emancipation act of 1829 was in thanksgiving to his Irish soldiers. This 'Act' improved the wellbeing not only of Catholics in Ireland but Catholics all over the British Empire.

THE IRISH REBELLION 1798

The Modern Masonic constitution of 1723 opened the door for Jews who were Freemasons, to emancipate their Jewish Brothers by openly initiating them as full members of Freemasonry and thereafter Freemasons and Jews virtually became a unified body, which migrated to Europe and America. They established Jewish-Masonic states in America 1776 and in France 1789, and began a campaign to establish another Jewish-Masonic state in Ireland, using their tried and tested formula of rousing and arming the people, Protestants and Catholics, to jointly fight the British, in order to establish a Democratic Republic which would guarantee freedom of religion, liberty, equality and fraternity. They successfully raised, trained and armed a military force of two hundred thousand soldiers to engage the British Military Establishment believing they would succeed as the English Jews and Freemasons supported them.

However, in the midst of the Masonic-Jewish preparations for war in Ireland, King George III's son, the Prince of Wales, was initiated into Freemasonry and everything suddenly changed. Now that the Freemasons had a Nobel Brother at their head, they could achieve their dearest wish, to transform England into a Masonic State, which was their birth-place and had been their global Headquarters since 1717.

The English Civil War had established a precedent in 1658 that, an English monarch cannot govern without the consent of Parliament. This concept became legally established in 1688 as part of the Glorious Revolution. From that time the kingdom of England, as well as its successor state, the United Kingdom, functioned in effect as a constitutional monarchy. On 1st May 1707, under the terms of the Acts of Union, the kingdoms of England and Scotland united to form the Kingdom of Great Britain.

The Modern Freemasonry constitution clause which committed them to maintain a protestant monarch on the Throne of England gave, comfort to the Prince of Wales who understood that, henceforth, he and his descendants would be strictly figureheads, subject to the will of the Democratic Government of England.

In about 1795 the Prince of Wales and his Masonic-Jewish brothers began secret negotiations to establish a formula to preserve the monarchy into the future, in order to keep the people who revered the Monarch in a state of happiness whilst the 'Brethren' governed the Union. Having come to terms with the Prince of Wales, the Masonic Jewish Alliance secretively set about expanding the existing union with Scotland and Wales to include Ireland and thereby establish England, Ireland, Scotland and Wales, as a single unified Masonic State.

The Irish Freemasons were delighted with news of the forthcoming Union but what were they going to do with about one hundred thousand Catholic volunteers, who were all fired up for a war with England? They secretively informed the Protestant Volunteers that the proposed war with England was called off because the English had offered everything the Protestant people hoped to achieve, however, they were warned them to keep it quite because the Catholic Volunteers will never accept English rule in Ireland. The Irish and English Masons conspired to entice as many as possible Irish Catholic Volunteers, into the British Army by offering them good pay rates and favourable conditions and then sent them away, to perform military duties through-out the empire, before the news of the'Union' finally broke. Not all of the volunteers signed up for military duties in the British Army. The protestant volunteers were largely recruited into the local militias and prepared to deal with the inevitable Catholic back-lash. The militias therefore had the advantage of knowing which Catholics had been trained in the use of arms and when the back-lash finally came in 1798 the combined strength of the militias and British Army killed upwards to 30,000 people in South East Ireland and the people of County Wexford suffered most of all. Lord Eardley MP; Manasseh Lopes MP and David Ricardo a financier were among prominent English Jews at that time.

ROTHSCHILD BANK'S INVOLVEMENT IN WAR OF 1812

The Americans were eager to consolidate their independence from the British Empire once and for all and the British were angry because the Americans had purchased Louisiana from Napoleon enabling him to continue his war with England. By winning the war in 1783, the colonists took control of their own government. Yet America remained in debt to the Jewish Goldsmids, Mocattas and the Oppenheimers, (all powerful Jewish families with interests of the gold trade), led by Nathan Mayer Rothschild. Benjamin Franklin who was quite knowledgeable of the European central banking system was against the establishment of a US central bank, along with Jefferson and Andrew Jackson... however in 1791 he died and that same year Alexander Hamilton who had close ties with the Rothschild Bank, had been trying to pass legislation for the first US central bank, he eventually succeeded in that same year of 1791, however in 1811 the banking charter for the US central bank expired and Nathan Rothschild threatened the Americans, **"Either the application for renewal of the charter is granted, or the United States will find itself involved in a most disastrous war."**

The United States stood firm and the Charter was not renewed. Nathan Mayer Rothschild then issued a command to the British, **"Teach those impudent Americans a lesson bring them back to colonial status."**

In 1812 backed by Rothschild money and on Nathan Mayer Rothschild's orders, the British declared war on the United States. Rothschild's plan was to cause the United States to build up such a debt in fighting this war that they would have to surrender to his demand, that the charter for the Rothschild owned First Bank of the United States be renewed. Nathan Rothschild's forecast became a reality following the end of the war when the treaty of Ghent was signed 24th December 1814 the US was heavily in debt and no option, but to renew the charter.

Many Jewish families made financial gains from the 1812 war and the Du Pont family who supplied gunpowder to the American Military is recognised as one of the top beneficiaries.

The bankers had calculated that the US would lose the war as the Americans were unprepared and the British were on course to win until they burned the White House and the government buildings in Washington. The British thought the destruction of the Capital would take the wind out of the American sails but it had the opposite effect, in that it ignited an indignant fury that rallied the American people who joined the army in their thousands, bringing the war to the British halting their progress and gained immortality when they heroically defended Fort McHenry inspiring Francis Scott Keys to record the battle poetically in 'The Star Spangled Banner' destined to become the National Anthem of the USA.

During the war, both sides suffered many losses. The British were quite defensive in the beginning, since they concentrated their military efforts on Napoleonic Wars but after their victory over France in 1815, they started to fight Americans more aggressively. American national pride was boosted by the victories in the Battle of Baltimore in 1814 and the Battle of New Orleans in 1815. Thanks to those victories the Americans started to call this war "a second war for independence". The Americans might have been defeated but when the British destroyed the Capital and burned the White House they effectively mobilised the American people who joined the army and navy en masse. By the end of 1812 privateers had stung more than 300 British merchantmen, most sailing off the North American coast or in the West Indies. Americans burned about 10 percent of the vessels they captured that were of little value, too easily recaptured or lacking prize crews. Another 10 percent sailed for English ports carrying British seamen being exchanged for American prisoners held in Britain. The remainder turned their bows to American ports, though some ran afoul of British warships—perhaps as much as 20 percent—while others disappeared in bad weather or wrecked on ironbound coasts. Still, the remaining merchantmen and their cargos poured wealth into coastal towns. American district courts condemned ships, fittings and goods, to be sold at auction, the proceeds shared per contract. Sailors, captured money weighing their pockets, rollicked through ports, happily trickling their hard-earned wealth into other hands and their war stories into other ears. But the big windfall went to investors and ship owners, who held their money close or invested it in new privateering enterprises. In Baltimore and other towns, artisans, journeymen and small merchants (the common man and woman) joined wealthier individuals in investing in the next wave of privateers.

The Jewish community acquired two important benefits from the War of 1812.

From American independence until the War of 1812, the state of Maryland explicitly required all citizens to make a Christian oath in order to hold office– a *de facto* exclusion of Jews from public service. Due to the documented heroism of Maryland Jewish soldiers in the War of 1812, the "Jew Bill" was passed in 1826, removing the requirement and opening the door for two Jewish men to be elected to the Baltimore City Council. Uriah Levy, the first Jewish commodore in the US Navy, played a major role in the War of 1812 before his capture by the British. Following the Treaty of Ghent, he rose to prominence in the Navy, and in

1834 bought Thomas Jefferson's Monticello estate in order to preserve it for historical purposes.

"The War of 1812 and the Jews: Beyond the Esplanade" by Dan Brosgol

https://www.jewishboston.com/read/the-war-of-1812-and-the-jews-beyond-the-esplanade/

THE SPANISH CIVIL WAR OF 1820

To understand the Spanish Civil War of 1936, it is necessary to study the Spanish Civil War of 1820. The Jewish Masonic Revolution that was released in France in 1789 was not an isolated affair. It was a continuation of Masonic revolutionary plan to financially enslave the whole world, that was first used in the American War of Independence.

Following the French Revolution, Rothschild money financed Grand Orient Freemasonry to establish a special school to train members for future International Masonic Revolutions. The Knights Templars, who were associates of the Freemasons, had shown that a small group of dedicated people could control monarchs by austerely managing a country's finances. The Templars became financial dictators and they also had the military expertize to enforce their edicts. King Philip IV of France was deeply in debt to the Templars and following a successful appeal to Pope Clement V in 1307 to dissolve the Templars, he ordered the arrest of French Templars and the execution of their leader, Grand Master, Jacques de Molay. Consequently, it is an objective of Freemasonry to overthrow, "both throne and altar on the tomb of Jacques de Molay". Albert Pike. Morals and Dogma. 1871, p. 824. This means to overthrow Catholic monarchies, the

Catholic Church and the Papacy. The Catholic Church calls all nations to holiness, love and justice. Dominum Mundi (Master of the World) was the Catholic order of state and church, subject to the Kingship of Jesus Christ, which is the basis of Western Civilization.

The Spanish Legislative Assembly (the Cortez) in 1812, having been infiltrated by crypto Jews, voted for a Trieno constitution that recognised King Ferdinand VII as the King of Spain but it contained provisions that were not in keeping with the magisterium of the Church. The new constitution also provided for unregulated economics and banking, guaranteeing that the market would be free to regulate itself. Apostolic Law would never operate such a constitution. The market should have checks, balances and fair laws to ensure that Money Power could never rule and dominate the economy by making its own laws.

King Ferdinand and the Catholic Church were alarmed at the proposed Money provisions of the Trieno. He and the Church were responsible before God to maintain a just economy for the good of the entire nation. He used his executive constitutional power of veto to cancel the Trieno that the Jews and the Masons had drawn up. The revolutionary forces assembled by Jews and Masons retaliated by arresting the King and keeping him hostage and initiating a civil war throughout the Spanish Nation.

The Catholic Church's appeal for assistance of other nations helped King Ferdinand's nephew to raise an army of 100,000 Sons of St Louis together with the intervention of French Catholics. They invaded Spain and defeated the revolutionaries and restored King Ferdinand. Histories of the 1820 Spanish Civil War invariably categories the measures used by King Ferdinand and his Catholic government as severe while defeating the combined Masonic and Jewish revolution. Spain and the Catholic Church is habitually vilified in historical accounts, because they took up arms against the Masonic and Jewish militants.

THE SPANISH CIVIL
WAR OF 1936-1939

Following the Civil War of 1820 the Spanish people lived ordinary lives in sporadic periods of peace, until the Jews and their Masonic friends won a majority of votes in local elections and declared a 'Spanish Republic' following the abdication of King Alfonso XIII in1931. They widely published their great achievement of freeing the people of Spain from their so-called Catholic Fascist oppressors, initiating a violent campaign against King Alfonso XIII, the Catholic people and their Church. The campaign began in Madrid, Seville and other cities. The government was slow to respond to the outbreak and that slowness left many of its opponents even more angry and suspicious than before. Spanish reformers had long sought to bring the country into the 20th century. Now it was clear that for the people governing Spain, that meant suppressing the Catholic Church. Random acts of anti-Catholic violence now became common. In Andalusia, after lightning destroyed a church roof and the priest celebrated Mass under the open sky, he was fined for an unauthorized public display of religion. Another priest, preaching on the feast of Christ the King, was fined for expressing monarchist sentiments by referring to the kingship of God. The ringing of church bells drew a fine in one place, while elsewhere churches were robbed and burned, with the authorities doing little to identify perpetrators. These are but a few of widespread anti-Catholic exploits, Catholics had to endure between 1931 and 1936.

Meanwhile, a reaction against the radical policies of the new regime was setting in among monarchists, aristocrats, wealthy people and the middle class, elements of the army and some in the Church. The conservative political parties pulled themselves together and began winning elections, while their opponents on the left grew ever more hostile and determined to fight if it came to that.

However, the left succeeded in winning the general election of the 23rd February 1936 and once again they used their crypto methods, to cause confusion among the electorate, convincing them to vote for a left wing coalition government, made up of Popular Front, socialists, communists, Accio Catalana, the Republican Party and the Spanish Socialist Party. Many of the elected members of the new parliament were Jews and Freemasons. This victory emboldened the left and a fresh wave of violence towards Catholics began almost at once.

Beleaguered Catholics had been asking for a long time, if the Spanish Army could help them. The answer came 17th July with an uprising among army units in Spanish Morocco under the command of Gen. Francisco Franco. The 1936 – 1939 Spanish Civil War was now in force.

Persecution of Catholics and destruction of Catholic churches, monasteries, schools, homes and confiscation of Catholic property continued for the duration of the war, mostly in the cities where republican forces and militias were in control. The leftists were a comprisal of elements from the Spanish Army, Jews, Freemasons, communists and mercenary criminals and they executed 12 Catholic Bishops, together with 6820 priests, nuns, monks and other clerics in the course of the war

It is estimated that 10,000 Jews from 53 countries held dominant military positions in the International Brigade's campaign to defeat Franco's army in the Spanish Civil War of 1936 – 1939. The international Jewry were also active in fund raising and supporting the Republican Army by publishing positive propaganda praising the government side while publishing constant negative and false propaganda to discredit Franco and his army.

Here is a list of some of the prominent Jews who served in the International Brigade, there are no records of Jews serving with Franco.

Leiba Lazarevich Felbin (Aleksandr Orlov): Chief of Soviet Security in the Spanish Civil War. He supervised massacres of Catholic priests and nuns.

Rabbi Hyman Katz: American rabbi. He said he joined Stalin's International Brigade "to fight Spanish-Christian fascists".

Milton wolff: Last commander of the American contingent of Stalin's International Brigade.

Abraham Osheroff: American Jewish Communist. Born in Brooklyn NY.

Olek Nuss: Yiddish poet. He severed with the *Naftali-Botwin Jewish Company.*

Janek Barvinski: Commander of the *Naftali-Botwin Jewish Company.*

Stach Matuszczak: Political Commissar of the *Naftali-Botswin Jewish Company.*

George Nathan: Jewish Communist from Great Britain. Chief of Staff of Stalin's International Bigrade.

Henryk Toruncxyk: Polish Jew. Commander of the *Naftali-Botwin Jewish Company.*

Saul Wellman: Commissar of the Abraham Lincoln Brigade. Communist activist from Detroit. Organized Communist party meetings amongst Detroit auto workers.

Kurt Julius Goldstein: German Jewish Communist.

Leon Rosenthal: A New York Jew. He was Stalin's propaganda agent in Spain.

Moses Rosenberg: The Russian Ambassador to Madrid. He rigged the elections of the Spanish Parliament in 1936 installing puppets of the Jewish Bolssheviks.

Jewish and Masonic efforts to establish another Masonic republic in Spain was planned to bring 24million Spanish people into the Jewish financial concentration camp.

This is the order to which Catholic Spain, monarchy and people belonged in 1820 and afterwards. Spain was a Catholic Nation founded by Saint James the Apostle. The Jews and the Freemasons planned to destroy it when they unleashed their revolutionary forces in 1820. Jesus Christ has always been an anathema to the Jews and in this day and age He is marginalized and dismissed in the Jewish controlled Media in the same manner as they dismiss anyone who criticizes them, as crazy conspiracy theorists.

THE IRISH IN THE AMERICAN-MEXICAN WAR 1845-1846

Flowing through Waterford Harbour is the confluence of the rivers, Barrow, Nore and Suir. The course of the confluence flows between the county boundaries of Wexford and Waterford, this great volume of water collides with Atlantic waves at the mouth of the harbour, generating deadly rip-currents in the process. In olden times when masters were guiding their vessels into the harbour they relied on strong winds to fill their sails and produce the necessary momentum for them to negotiate the perilous cross currents. However, the most dangerous currents were and still are in the centre of the harbour, so it was essential to maintain a course either to the left or to right of centre where the slack waters lie. The Hook light-house stands on the Wexford side of the harbour and Crooke Village is located on the Waterford side. Consequently, local seafarers learned that it was vital to proceed by the Hook side or by the Crooke side, to safely enter Waterford Harbour. Hence, developed the popular saying, "By hook or by crook

Seafaring conditions along Wexford's Atlantic coast can be challenging and many famous seafarers developed their sea-legs on these waters. It is reported that Lord

Nelson said, "Give me a crew of Wexford farmers and I will face any foe", due to fact that it was well known that Wexford famers, fished these water during the farming 'off season'. The most famous seafarers from the Wexford are: Commodore John Barry of Southeast Wexford, he enlisted in George Washington's Navy during the American War Of Independence and he was later appointed the first commissioned officer in the United States Navy, He is popularly known as the father of the American Navy. Admiral David Beatty of Killurin, outside Wexford town, joined the Royal Navy. He was famously involved in the Battle of Jutland in 1916 and he was eventually promoted as the First Sea Lord in London. Admiral Robert McClure of Wexford town was a first cousin of Oscar Wilde. He became an artic explorer and eventually found the final link of the Northwest Passage, a part of which bears his name, 'The McClure Strait'. William Lamport from the Southeast of Wexford County, was born into a noble Irish family in 1615 and was educated by Jesuits in Dublin and London. He too acquired his sea going experience on the Wexford Coast. He was forced leave Ireland for his own safety, following his expression of anti-English sentiments, he joined the Spanish Navy. He fought in the Spanish 17th century wars against France and his bravery was noted by the Duke of Olivares, chief minister at the court of Philip IV of Spain. Some years later he was sent to Mexico to escape scandal following a liaison with a Spanish noble woman. There the Inquisition accused him of conspiring against Spain, when he advocated the liberation Indians and black slaves and declaring himself to be the leader of an Independent Mexico. He was sentenced to be burnt at the stake but he managed to strangle himself with the rope that bound him to the stake before he was burned in 1659. He is remembered as the patriot who started the Mexican Independence movement, which finally gained independence from Spain in 1821. His statute is in the Parliament building in Mexico City where Don Guillén de Lampart is remembered as the original San Patricio. Some believe that Johnston McCulley's book 'Zorro' is based on William Lamport's life and times.

Other notables having Wexford roots: Include, John F. Kennedy US President, Buffalo Bill Cody, James Bolger Prime Minister New Zealand, Sir Arthur Conan Doyle, Oscar Wilde, Francis Danby artist, Major Myles Keogh who died at the battle of the Little Big Horn, Guglielmo Marconi (wireless telegraphy) lived with his mother Anne Jameson of the 'Jameson Whiskey family in the Wexford town of Enniscorthy

Wexford People Migrate en masse to Refugio in the state of Texas.

Following the Irish rebellion of 1798 the people of County Wexford were harassed, severely punished, evicted from their homes and lands leaving them annually on the verge of starvation. When the people of Ballygarrett and surrounding area, heard that the Mexican Government was offering 1000 acres of land free of charge, to settlers to colonise the virgin Refugio territory in Texas, they saw it as an opportunity to escape from persecution and famine. Many of them eagerly signed up to be included in the scheme even though it meant separation from family, friends and relations forever.

In 1833 James Power organized and led a group of six hundred people from Wexford in a mass migration to Refugio, under a scheme approved by the Mexican jurisdiction in Mexico's state of Texas, to colonise vacant lands in Refugio. The first group departed in December 1832 and the second in January 1833. Their journey took them to Liverpool where they boarded ships bound for New Orleans, some of the migrants perished en route during the slow and torturous sail voyages of that time. Having arrived in New Orleans some of them died from an outbreak of cholera and they were buried in Louisiana on the banks of the Mississippi River. The survivors made their way to Copano Bay with their crude implements and other belongings. Even then their woes were not over. One of their boats capsized in Copano Bay with the loss of much of their goods. The Wexford people having left home as a result of the Irish Freemasonry Revolution of 1798 were soon to be embroiled in another Freemasonry war of independence.

The Mexican democratic government had been usurped by this time and the new military dictator, General Antonio Lopez de Santa Anna, declared the land contracts, signed by his predecessors to be null and void. Santa Anna was a Freemason and he correctly suspected that President James Knox Polk and his masonic friends were covertly supporting and directing American settlers to apply for land settlements with the intention of suing for independence from Mexico when they had amassed a resident army of settlers. They greedily wanted to add Texas to their land bank. (Masons and Zionists used this formula to settle Jews in Palestine in preparation for the establishment of the State of Israel in 1948 and they have continued to steal land from Palestine and Syria)

In 1835, settlers from the United States who lived in Texas formed a provisional government, and in 1836 called for independence. In turn, the Mexican government deployed the Mexican leader **Antonio Lopez de Santa Anna** and his troops into the region in an effort to regain political control.

Santa Anna speedily arrived on Texas soil to drive out the American backed settlers but the settlers were well organised and armed and Santa Anna encountered stiff resistance from the Texas Revolutionaries, and he failed to eliminate them conclusively. The Mexican–American War confirmed Texas's southern border at the Rio Grande, indicating the United States victory. The United States also acquired California, New Mexico, and Arizona, as well as parts of Nevada, Utah, Colorado and Wyoming The settlers declared their independence from Mexico in 1836 and the New Texas government legalized slavery and demanded recognition from President Jackson and annexation into the United States. Mexico refused to recognize the independence of the Republic of Texas and intermittent conflicts between the two states continued into the 1840s. The United States recognized the Republic of Texas in 1837 but 'decently' declined to annex Texas at that time, however, the ground work was done and annexation could wait for the appropriate occasion.

The people from Wexford who had settled in Refugio were caught up in the American Mexican dispute and they had to make difficult decisions regarding their loyalty to Mexico or to the American invaders. One source says that thirteen Irish born and many more with Irish connections including Jim Bowie, Davy Crockett and Col. William B Travis died in the Battle of the Alamo. The Wexford people in the Refugio area survived and multiplied and their descendants are still very much in evidence in that part of Texas and their traditional presence there is recognized in the Spanish named 'San Patricio County'. (St Patrick's County).

Ireland's Holocaust by Famine

The Irish famine really began when the ethnic Irish Catholics were reduced to stone-age living conditions as a result of English Masonic hatred towards them. The native Irish people were forced to live in hovels on small parcels of land on which they cultivated potatoes that became their stable food. The potato being the main ingredient in their diet proved to be very wholesome and the Irish Catholic people became a very healthy race. A population explosion occurred reaching a total of more than eight million people in the 1830s. The population in England at that time was twenty-four million.

Early in the 1840s a fungus developed in some potato crops destroying many of the tubers and each succeeding year thereafter destruction increased causing localized famine and the total potato crop was wiped out in 1847 bringing widespread famine. People died in hundreds of thousands, and others in fear and great despair gathered all they had and left Ireland in thousands. Between 1846 and 1850 more than three million people either died or emigrated and in the succeeding years another million and one half departed. Many went to England, Wales and Scotland, while others sailed to the USA and Canada. Ireland's population decreased and remained below four million until the 1980s.

Following the reformation which King Henry VIII imposed on Catholic England, the Catholic working class was wiped out and it was Irish famine migrants who re-established a Catholic working class in England in the 1850s.

At that time the American Army had a practice sending their recruiting staff to meet the Irish Famine Ships and the young men disembarking were approached and welcomed to the USA and offered positions in the military. These traumatized young men were hungry, lost, lonely, and tired from the hazards of the journey, were very pleased to accept an offer of food, uniforms, a place to sleep, foot-ware, promises of land grants and they would also be paid with real money.

The new recruits were taken to army barracks where they were kitted out and began a program of basic military training and they were soon to discover that it was not a bed of roses in the American army. Nevertheless, they were already familiar with the harsh conditions of living under Protestant Landlords while growing up in Ireland and they knew they had to endure the hostility of Irish Protestant officers in the American Army had for Irish Catholic soldiers, for it closely resembled the insolent attitude of the authorities back home in Ireland. Following a period of army training they were ready to use the military skills they had leaned in camp and engage a real enemy.

American – Mexican War 1846-1848

The Irish troops were then transported to the American Mexico border to fight in the war, which Freemasonry President James K. Polk had declared on Mexico. He controversially believed in the so called 'Manifest Destiny' mission to redeem the Old World and to establish a New and better World. The badly trained and badly equipped Mexican army was not a real match for the Americans, who took great pleasure in dispatching Mexican Catholic soldiers from south of the border. Irish Catholic soldiers in the American army were appalled at the slaughter of poorly equipped Mexican Catholic soldiers. It brought back memories of the savage unmerciful tactics of the British Army, during and after the Irish Rebellion of 1798, which left many parts of Ireland devoid of young men.

A historical account exists of a situation, where Irish soldiers were entrenched overlooking a village on the Mexican side. They could hear the church bell ringing as the people assembled for Mass and a number of the soldiers decided to attend. When they arrived at the church they were arrested by the Mexican army who threatened to shoot them. The Irish soldiers were able to explain that they too were Catholics and that they did not approve of the American invasion into Mexico. The Mexicans then suggested, if they were to join the Mexican army they would receive commissions, better wages and land grants when the war was over.

John Patrick Riley 1817-1850 was an Irish Catholic soldier in the American Army. He led a number of his Irish Catholics comrades from the ranks to defect and join the Mexican army, where he formed St Patrick's battalion, which gallantly fought with the Mexicans until Mexico surrendered. Many of the defectors in St Patrick's Battalion (San Patricios) had been trained in the use of artillery and their knowledge of field guns helped the battalion to hold key positions in various battles. This battalion served as an artillery unit for much of the war and in many ways, acted as the sole Mexican counterbalance to the recent U.S. innovation of horse artillery. The "San Patricios" were responsible for the toughest battles encountered by the United States during its invasion of Mexico, with Ulysses S. Grant remarking that "Churubusco proved to be about the severest battle fought in the valley of Mexico". Irish soldiers serving with the Mexicans are said to have concentrated their rifle fire on the abusive American officers, rather than the men in ranks, who might be neighbours from Ireland.

When Mexico surrendered the Americans rounded up as many members of "St Patrick's Battalion as they could find and cruelly hung fifty of them at the same time, having refused the Irishmen's request to be executed by firing squad in traditional Military fashion. Those who were spared were branded on the cheek with the letter 'D' to signify deserter. The U.S. army held an investigation into the cause of the Irishmen's action and concluded that the army's failure to provide spiritual support for the soldiers was the reason they left the American lines in the first place. The American Army thereafter made sure, that priority would be given to the spiritual needs of their military personnel.

The provision of spiritual services for Christian soldiers in the USA and other western countries gave comfort to those who doubted the morality of being ordered to kill humans in order to preserve home and country. This policy is akin to the ancient Egyptian Pharaohs who convinced their people that the erection of temples and pyramids pleased the Gods and secured an afterlife.

Unfortunately, Middle-Eastern and Asian countries see western militarism as Christian aggression and Christian communities in these countries are now judged as enemies and are frequently persecuted.

For Mexicans, the "San Patricios" were and still are the heroes, who came to their aid in an hour of need. Emotional memories of the Irishmen's gallant efforts to secure justice and peace for the Mexican nation under siege will never be forgotten. St Patrick's Battalion has attained a very special place in the hearts, history and legends of the Mexican people..

Irishmen have traditionally married indigenous women in places where they settled. Two prominent examples are,

Anthony Quinn who had roots in County Cork and Che Guevara Lynch had roots in County Galway and many of the San Patricios married Mexican women.

A community of Mexican nuns held the San Patricos in great esteem for they made a banner for the Battalion, "A beautiful green silk banner, on which glittered a silver cross and a golden harp, embroidered by the hands of the fair nuns of San Luis Potois".

The Irish song writer, Jimmy Kennedy wrote the song, "South of the Border down Mexico way", which Gene Autry collected in Dublin, Ireland, where he gave a concert on 1st September 1939. When he returned to America his recording of this song was hugely popular and became an international evergreen. Kennedy was inspired to write this song when he received a postcard from his sister, while she was on a visit to Mexico. Some Irish people speculated that the man in the song was a San Patrico, on active duty and failing to return, his broken hearted lover assumed he had been killed in the war and she entered the convent and became a nun. A line in the song says, "He rode back one day and there in a veil of white by candle light she knelt to pray, the mission bells told him he mustn't stay". It is an Irish tradition that a nun's marriage to God is sacrosanct and demands utmost respect.

MONEY AND CIVIL WAR
IN AMERICA 1861-1865

Twenty-six years before the outbreak of the civil war there was an economic depression in America because there was a shortage of money for development.

President Andrew Jackson regarded the Second Bank of the United States as a corrupt institution, that benefited the wealthy at the expense of ordinary Americans and he vetoed the renewal of its charter. After a lengthy campaign Jackson and his allies thoroughly dismantled the Second Bank. In 1835, Jackson became the only president to completely pay off the national debt, fulfilling a long time goal but he caused consternation in London.

Rothschilds panicked when Jackson vetoed the proposal to re-charter their bank and set in motion their plan to execute him. A public assassination was their favourite method of sending an important message. However, Jackson had a Premonition and sent a letter to Vice President Van Buren saying, "The bank is trying to kill me, but I will kill it". Rothschilds hired Richard Lawrence an unemployed house painter, who was mentally unstable to do their dirty work. One wet and windy night in 1835, Lawrence waited near the steps of Capital building, as Jackson approached he pulled out his pistol and pulled the trigger but the pistol misfired. Jackson attacked the confused Lawrence, knocking him to the ground with his cane but Lawrence pulled another pistol aimed at Jackson and pulled the trigger but it too, misfired. Lawrence was sentenced to spend the rest of his life in a mental institution and before he died he admitted, that powerful people from England had hired him to kill the President.

Slave trading

Historians are divided as to the extent of Jewish ownership of slaves and of Jewish bankers involvement in slave trading before the Civil War but scrutiny of financial records, have revealed some strong evidence of relationships between slave traders, slave owners and Jewish owned banks.

Research has shown the Jews did own some slaves but profit from loans they gave to slave owners and slaves traders was enormous. New York's financial district was the site of one of the US' largest slave markets. It was enslaved people who built the wall after which Wall Street is named. Some estimate New York received up to 40% of US cotton revenue from the money its financial firms, shipping businesses and insurance companies earned. Enslaved people were bought to work on cotton, sugar and tobacco plantations. The crops they grew were sent to Europe and some to the northern colonies, to be converted into consumer products. British profits were made from exporting manufactured goods to Africa and importing slave products such as sugar. Ports such as Glasgow, Bristol and Liverpool prospered as a result of the slave trade. The finished goods were used to fund further trips to Africa to capture more slaves, who were then transported back and sold in America. This lucrative trading route was very profitable for investors. In order to raise money to finance the establishment of plantations and to buy slaves to work them, many future plantation owners turned to capital markets in London selling debt, that could be used to purchase ships, goods and slaves.

Up to the middle of the 19th Century, exports of raw cotton totalled more than half of US trading overseas. Surplus cotton was sold to mills in Massachusetts and Rhode Island to be turned into fabric. The money southern plantation owners earned was deposited in US banks and enslaved people counted as assets when assessing a person's wealth. Some US banks have made public apologies for the role they played in slavery.

In 2005, the biggest bank in the US, JP Morgan Chase, admitted that enslaved people were accepted as collateral by its subsidiaries; Citizens Bank and Canal Bank in Louisiana. If the slave owners defaulted on loan payment the banks took ownership of the listed slaves.

JP Morgan was not alone. The predecessors of Citibank, Bank of America and Wells Fargo are among a list of other

US financial companies that benefited from the slave trade. Slavery was the backbone of both the British and the US economies at that time.

Early in the 19th Century, United States banks and Southern States sold securities to fund the enlargement of plantations. To eliminate risks involved in transporting unwilling slaves across the Atlantic to America, the traders purchased insurance policies. Some large insurance companies in the US such as, New York Life, Aetna and AIG sold policies that insured slave owners against the loss of slaves, due to injury or death resulting from accidents whilst in transit.

"The hidden links between slavery and Wall Street".

https://www.bbc.com/news/business-49476247#:~: text=In%202005%2C%20JP%20Morgan%20Chase,JP%20 Morgan%20was%20not%20alone.

Reported in the Financial Times, "Documents from the British National Archives reveal that Rothschild founder, Nathan Mayer Rothschild used slaves as collateral in a bank deal with a slave owner and James William Freshfield, founding partner of Freshfields, acted as a trustee in deals involving Caribbean slave plantations". Revelations have been unearthed, as part of a three-year long research project, to look at the legacy of British slave ownership and understand how slavery helped to shape modern Britain and the USA. The compensation records also act as a census, of the 3,000 to 5,000 slave owners of three million slaves in the British Empire in the 1830s *"Top UK City firm founders linked to slavery"* https://www.antislavery.org/top-uk-city-firm-founders-linked-slavery/

President Lincoln's Greenbacks

Abraham Lincoln said "Labor is prior to, and independent of, capital. Capital is only the fruit of labor, and could never have existed if labor had not first existed. Labor is the superior of capital, and deserves much the higher consideration. Capital has its rights, which are as worthy of protection as any other rights. Nor is it denied that there is, and probably always will be, a relation between labor and capital, producing mutual benefits. The error is in assuming that the whole labor of the community exists within that relation. …. In most of the southern States, a majority of the whole people of all colors are neither slaves nor masters; while in the northern a large majority are neither, hirers nor hired".

"Many independent men everywhere in these States, a few years back in their lives, were hired laborers. The prudent, penniless beginner in the world, labors for wages awhile, saves a surplus with which to buy tools or land for himself; then labors on his own account another while, and at length hires another new beginner to help him. This is the just, and generous, and prosperous system, which opens the way to all, gives hope to all, and consequent energy, and progress, and improvement of condition to all. No men living are more worthy to be trusted than those who toil up from poverty – none less inclined to take, or touch, aught that they have not honestly earned. Let them beware of surrendering a political power which they already possess, and which, if surrendered, will surely be used to close the door of advancement against such as they are, and to fix new disabilities and burdens upon them, till all of liberty shall be lost".

At the beginning of the US Civil War the national debt was $65 million, towards the end of the War the national debt was approaching $5.2 billion. President Lincoln needed more money to finance the Civil War, and the private syndicated banks offered him loans at 24-36% interest. Lincoln balked at their demands because he didn't want to plunge the nation into such a huge debt. Lincoln approached Congress about passing a law to authorize the printing of U.S. Treasury Notes. Lincoln said "We gave the people of this Republic the greatest blessing they ever had - their own paper money to pay their debts..." Lincoln printed over 400 million "Greenbacks" (debt and interest-free) and paid the soldiers, U.S. government employees, and bought war supplies.

The international bankers were furious with this new development as they wanted Lincoln to borrow the money from them and pay interest on the loans. Lincoln's solution made this seem ridiculous. Lincoln's public assassination was a message the government could not ignore and revoked the Greenback law, to end Lincoln's debt-free, interest-free money. A new national banking act was enacted at that time and all currency became private bank, interest-bearing debt instruments again.

Attributed quote from the bank of England in 1865: "If that mischievous financial policy, which had its origin in the North American Republic, should become indurated down to a fixture, then that government will furnish its own money without cost. It will pay off its debts and be without debt [to the international bankers]. It will become prosperous beyond precedent in the history of the civilized governments of the world. The brains and wealth of all countries will go to North America. That government must be destroyed or it will destroy every monarchy on the globe".

It seems Lincoln effectively signed his own death warrant when he authorised the printing of greenbacks.

JEWISH CONFLICTS
WITH GENTILES

There is a long history of Jewish association with money and wealth. Moses castigated his followers for adoring a golden calf. Solomon, the King of Israel who accumulated a vast empire of power and wealth inspires Jewish people who believe, their promised Messiah will be a Solomon like figure of great power and wealth.

Jesus Christ introduced a radical and moral philosophy which opposed Jewish philosophy regarding power and wealth and the business people were so horrified with this anathematic proposal that it was a cause for His crucifixion.

John 2:15, Describes the anger of Jesus as He drove the 'money changers' out of the temple. It seems, Jesus did not approve of wealthy Jews who loved of the power of money and had no compassion for those who borrowed money from them on condition that they pay interest on loans. He obviously considered the practice to be unholy, as it gave evil people the power to manipulate others. In this instance, He was warning His followers, that the abuse of money would destroy humanity and the world, if they did not wisely use money to do God's work, i.e. maintain one's family and fulfil the spiritual and temporal needs of everyone.

In the Gospel St. Mark 12:17, Jesus implied that the fruit of our labour should be used to do God's work, i.e. **the spiritual and the temporal works of mercy** and to provide civil amenities for the benefit of everyone. Any attempt to use the people's money for evil purposes is therefore absolutely taboo.

Historic conflict between Gentiles and Jews springs from the exacting financial oppression Jewish merchants place on gentiles who borrow money from them. These usury conditions generate fear, apprehension and social separation between Jewish bankers and Gentiles and the resultant animosity is known as anti-Semitism. The Jews are not primarily recorded for their generosity or as peacemakers they have rather the reputation of rabble-rousers, exploiters and initiators of conflicts among people and nations. The power of money was employed by the Jews to persuade Judas Iscariot to betray Jesus for thirty pieces of silver. Emperor Claudius issued his third Edict in AD41 condemning the Jews of Alexandria for abusing their privileges, sowing discord and fomenting false expectations of financial gains. Cassius Dio recorded his observation of the Jews causing a major war; "Jews everywhere were showing signs of hostility to the Romans, partly by secret and partly overt acts and many other nations joined them, eagerly expecting gains and the whole world was in a state of revolution".

Other notable Romans condemned the Jews, Seneca said, "They were an accursed race", Quintilian said "They are a race which is a curse to others" and Tacitus "They are a disease, a pernicious superstition and the basest of peoples".

The negative reputation of the Jews endured to the Renaissance, Thomas Aquinas, Martin Luther and John Chrysostom all condemned Jewish usury, a lending practice frequently making large profits on loans, to dis-advantaged and distressed people. Baron d'Holbach said. "The Jewish people distinguished themselves by massacres, unjust wars, cruelties, usurpations, infamies, living continually in the midst of calamities and were more than all other nations, the sport of frightful revolutions". Voltaire was struck by the danger posed to humanity by the Hebrew tribe, "I would not be in the least bit surprised if these people would not some day become deadly to the human race". Kant called them, "a nation of deceivers", and Hegel said, "The only act Moses reserved for Israelites was, to borrow with deceit and repay confidence with theft".

Jewish Advance in America and Elsewhere

The history of Jewish involvement in social conflict has had a direct bearing on both world wars. Their influence on American governance began before the American War of Independence. In 1845, the first Jews were elected; Lewis Levin (PA) to the House and David Yulee (FLA) to the Senate, Washington Barlett as Governor of California and in 1889 President Harrison appointed Solomon Hirsch as ambassador to the Ottoman Empire, that controlled Palestine at that time.

In Russia in 1881 a gang of anarchists which included some Jews killed Czar Alexander II. This unleashed series of pogroms killing hundreds of Jews and the 'May Laws of 1882' placed restrictions on Jewish businesses and areas of residences within the "Pale of Settlement" in the western part of Russian Empire, from where many of the Russian Jews fled to Germany.

Jewish numbers and influence in Germany before the 1880s was considerable. Karl Marx and Bruno Bauer wrote influential essays on the Jewish Question (Die Judenfrage) in the 1840s. In 1850 Richard Wagner the composer complained that "Germans needed to be emancipated from the Jews. The Jew is, in fact more than emancipated... He rules" Wagner later declared, "Jewish control of German newspapers was almost total". In 1879 Wilhelm Marr lamented, "The victory of Jewry over Germandom" was achieved, "Without striking a blow...Jewry today has become the socio-political dictator of Germany". In addition, there was an influx of Russian and Polish Jews towards the end of the 19th century and the early part of the 20th century and Jews gained a great many positions in the higher echelons of German society. The records of that time confirm the Jewish standing in Germany:

Before world war one, Jews occupied 13 percent of the directorships of joint-stock corporations and 24 percent of the supervisory positions within these corporations. In 1904 they comprised 27 percent of all lawyers, 10 percent of all apprenticed lawyers, 5 percent of court clerks, 4 percent of magistrates and up to 30 percent of all higher ranks of the judiciary. Jews were overrepresented among university professors and students between 1870 and 1933. For example, in 1909-1910 almost 12 percent of instructors at German universities were Jewish. In 1905-1906 Jewish students comprised 25 percent of the law and medical students. The percentage of Jewish doctors was also quite high, especially in large cities, where they were sometimes a majority. In Berlin around 1890, 25 percent of all children attending grammar school were Jewish. In all this Jews never exceeded 2 percent of the German population. The public accepted the Jews with a remarkable tolerance and more or less allowed them to dominate certain sectors of German society. There were no legal constraints and violent attacks were rare. But the Germans would come to regret such liberal policies.

In 1897 Theodor Herzl established the basic principle of Zionism in his book 'Der Judenstaat' (the Jewish State). He stated that the Jews would never be free from persecution until they had their own state. The World Zionist Organisation held its first meeting in 1897 in Basel Switzerland and settled on Palestine which included Gaza, Jerusalem and the Golan heights. This presented a problem because the region was under the control of the Ottoman Empire and was mainly populated with Muslims and Christian Arabs. However the Zionist Jews decided to embark on secret program to wrench Palestine away from the Ottomon Turks and expel the Arabs, in spite of projected impossible difficulties. They agreed that this could only be done by force. It would take something like a world war to enable the Zionists to initiate their guiding principle **'profit through distress'** and then manipulate things to their advantage. In states where they had influence, they would use the power of their accumulated wealth to dictate national policy. In states where they had neither population nor influence, they would apply external pressure to secure support for their purposes. In fact Herzl apparently predicted the outbreak of global war. One of the original Zionists, Litman Rosenthal wrote in his diary of 15th December 1914 his recollection of a conversation with Herzl who said; **It may be that Turkey will refuse to understand us. This will not discourage us. We will seek other means to accomplish our end. The Orient is now the question of the day. Sooner or later it will bring a conflict among the nations. A European war is imminent the great European war must come. With my watch in my hand do I await this terrible moment. After the great European war is ended the Peace Conference will assemble. We must be ready for that time. We will assuredly be called to this great**

conference of the nations and we must prove to them the urgent importance of a Zionist solution to the Jewish Question". His prophecy of a great European war suggests that he had prior knowledge of the factors that were in place to ignite that terrible conflict. Was he party to the financing of the production of necessary military material to engage an enemy?

In spite of the many difficulties, the Zionists envisioned in 1897 to annex the whole of Palestine, (they have yet to conquer Gaza and all of Jerusalem). It has taken them 123 years to establish the State of Israel as of 2020, the death and displacement of many thousands of Arabs and turning Gaza into a vast concentration camp. Since their illegal occupation of Palestine in 1948 the Israelis have shown little sympathy, compassion or diplomacy towards the Arabs, preferring always to use violence to keep the peace. General Moshe Dayan said. "Israel must invent dangers, and to do this it must adapt the strategy of provocation and revenge".

Israeli Prime Minister, David Ben Gurion said in a letter to son in 1937. "We must expel the Arabs and take their place. In each attack a decisive blow should be struck resulting in the destruction of homes and the expulsion of the population". Israel invented a policy of exclusive Jewish traditional rights to the Holy Land that, permitted them to use every possible means, to engage in creeping ethnic cleansing to wipe out the entire Arab population from Palestine.

By the first half of 1949, at least 750,000 Palestinians in total were forcibly expelled or fled from their homeland. Zionist forces had committed about 223 atrocities by 1949, including massacres, attacks such as bombings of homes, looting, the destruction of property and entire villages.

What is the situation today? Palestinians living in occupied West and East Jerusalem face home demolitions, arbitrary arrests and displacement as Israel expands the 100-plus Jewish-only colonies stealing Palestinian land to do so. Palestinian movement is restricted by military checkpoints and the Separation Wall has obstructed their ability to travel freely and work on their own land.

Today, there are more than 7.98 million Palestinian refugees and internally displaced persons who are barred from returning to their original homes and villages in Israel and the illegally annexed territory

Some 6.14 million of those are refugees and their descendants are living beyond the borders of Israel in atrocious conditions in more than 50 refugee camps run by the UN in neighbouring countries.

The population Israel before its independence comprised of 61% Arabs and 29% Jews, in 2019, 20.97% were Arabs and 74.24% were Jews. It is obvious that Israel's policy of ethnic cleansing is very effective.

The Masonic-Zionist association is the driver behind the Israeli State that ignores International Law and United Nations regarding Israel's oppression of Palestinians. It's unfortunate that Jewish people, who promote peace and fundamental human rights, are also tarred with the same brush that is used to tar Masons and Zionists.

WORLD WAR ONE 1914-1918

The Balfour Letter

The Zionist Federation informed the Allies that they were prepared to support them financially and in the media, which they largely controlled at home and internationally, on condition they would be given a concrete assurance of Allied support for a Jewish Home in Palestine. The Allies agreed to the Zionist's terms and the British Government issued the Balfour Letter:

> Foreign Office
> November 2nd, 1917

> Dear Lord Rothschild:

> I have much pleasure in conveying to you. on behalf of His Majesty's Government, the following declaration of sympathy with Jewish Zionist aspirations which has been submitted to, and approved by, the Cabinet:

> His Majesty's Government view with favour the establishment in Palestine of a national home for the Jewish people, and will use their best endeavours to facilitate the achievement of this object, it being clearly understood that nothing shall be done which may prejudice

the civil and religious rights of existing non-Jewish communities in Palestine, or the rights and political status enjoyed by Jews in any other country.

I should be grateful if you would bring this declaration to the knowledge of the Zionist Federation.

Yours,
Arthur James Balfour.

(Israel has named a street in Jerusalem to honour James Arthur Balfour).

Later the British Prime Minister, Lloyd George said; **"The Zionist leaders gave us a definite promise that, if the Allies committed themselves to a national home for the Jews in Palestine, they would do their best to rally Jewish sentiment and support throughout the world to the Allied cause. They kept their word".**

What is extraordinary about the Balfour letter is, the British did not occupy Palestine at that time, which raises the question: Did the British commitment to "use their best endeavours to facilitate the achievement of this object..." mean that they agreed to invade Palestine purely to provide a home for the Jews? A Churchill memo to his War Cabinet states; **"It was not for light or sentimental reasons Lord Balfour and the Government of 1917 made the** promises to the Zionists which have been the cause of so much subsequent discussion. The influence of American Jewry was rated then as a factor of the highest importance, and we did not feel ourselves in such a strong position as to be able to treat it with indifference".

The Plan to Involve America in World War One.

Masonic and Zionist plans to draw the United States into the war started on October 25, 1911, when Winston Churchill was appointed the First Lord of the Admiralty in England.

Winston Churchill's statement in 1920 appears to confirm that he was fully aware of the Masons and Zionist plans to restructure global society when he concluded that there was indeed a master conspiracy at work in all the major events throughout the world and perhaps he was one the so-called conspirators: *"This movement among the Jews is new From the days of Spartacus—Weishaupt to those of Karl Marx, and down to Trosky (Russia), Bela Kun (Hungary), Rosa Luxemburg (Germany), and Emma Goldman (United States).this world-wide conspiracy for the overthrow of civilization and for the reconstitution of society on the basis of arrested development, of envious malevolence, and impossible equality, has been steadily growing. It has been the mainspring of every subversive movement during the Nineteenth Century; and now at last this band of extraordinary personalities from the underworld, of the great cities of Europe and America, have gripped the Russian people by the hair of their heads and have become practically the undisputed masters of that enormous empire".* The Churchill you did'nt know….. The guardian.

The second key appointment made during the pre-war period was the appointment of Franklin Delano Roosevelt as Assistant Secretary of the US Navy by President Woodrow Wilson.

Roosevelt is also on record as concluding that there was a conspiracy, at least in the United States. He once wrote to Colonel Edward Mandell House: *"The real truth of the matter is, as you and I know, that a financial element in the larger centers has owned the government ever since the days of Andrew Jackson, and I am not wholly excepting the administration of W.W. (Woodrow Wilson.) The country is going through a repetition of Jackson's fight with the Bank of the United States—only on a far bigger and broader basis."*

THE SINKING OF THE LUSITANIA

The next step in the Masonic-Zionist scheme to bring the United States into the war came when the Cunard Lines, owners of the **Lusitania**, honoured a government financing agreement to make the liner available to the English Navy in times of war. The First Lord of the Admiralty, Winston Churchill, directed the Lusitania to secretly transport to England weapons, ammunition and other military paraphernalia, supplied by J.P. Morgan and Company in the USA, to be used by England and France in the war against Germany.

It was known that the very wealthy were interested in involving the American government in that war, and Secretary of State William Jennings Bryan was aware of the rumour. *"As Secretary [Bryan] had anticipated, the large banking interests were deeply interested in the World War because of wide opportunities for large profits. On August 3, 1914, even before the actual clash of arms, the French firm of Rothschild Freres cabled to Morgan and Company in New York suggesting the flotation of a loan of $100,000,000, a substantial part of which was to be left in the United States, to pay for French purchases of American goods."*

England broke the German war code on December 14, 1914, so that By the end of January, 1915, [British

Intelligence was] able to advise the Admiralty of the departure of each U-boat as it departed on patrol,

This meant that the First Lord of the Admiralty, Winston Churchill, knew where every U-boat was in the vicinity of the South Irish Sea and the English Channel.

The Lusitania was set to sail to England that was already at war with Germany. The German government had placed advertisements in the New York newspapers warning people considering whether or not to sail with the ship to England that they would be sailing into a war zone, and that the liner could be sunk.

Secretary Bryan promised that *"he would endeavour to persuade the President (Woodrow Wilson) publicly to warn the Americans not to travel [aboard the Lusitania]. No such warning was issued by the President, but there can be no doubt that President Wilson was told of the character of the cargo destined for the Lusitania. He did nothing...."*

Even though Wilson proclaimed America's neutrality in the European War in accordance with the prior admonitions of George Washington but his government was never-the-less secretly plotting to involve the American people by having the *Lusitania* sunk. This was made public in the book *The Intimate Papers of Colonel House*, written by a supporter of the Colonel, who recorded a conversation between Colonel House and Sir Edward Grey of England, the Foreign Secretary of England:

Grey: What will America do if the Germans sink an ocean liner with American passengers on board?

House: I believe that a flame of indignation would sweep the United States and that by itself would be sufficient to carry us into the war.

On May 7, 1915, the *Lusitania* was sunk off the coast of County Cork, Ireland by a U-boat after it had slowed to await the arrival of the English escort vessel, the *Juno*, which was intended to escort it into the English port. The First Lord of the Admiralty, Winston Churchill, issued orders that the Juno was to return to port, and the *Lusitania* sat alone in the channel. Because Churchill knew of the presence of three U-boats in the vicinity, it is reasonable to presume that he had planned for the *Lusitania* to be sunk, and it was. 1201 people lost their lives in the sinking.

This sinking has been described by Colin Simpson, the author of a book entitled *The Lusitania*, as "the foulest act of wilful murder ever committed on the seas."

But the event was not enough to enable President Wilson to declare war against the German government, and the conspirators changed tactics. They would use other means to get the American people involved in the war, as the "flame of indignation" did not sweep the United States as had been planned.

Robert Lansing, the Assistant Secretary of State, is on record as stating: "We must educate the public gradually — draw it along to the point where it will be willing to go into the war."

After the sinking of the *Lusitania*, two inquiries were held, one by the English government, in June, 1915, and one by the American government in 1918. Mr. Simpson has written that "Both sets of archives... contain meagre information. There are substantial differences of fact in the two sets of papers and in many cases it is difficult to accept that the files relate to the same vessel."

But in both inquiries, the conclusions were the same: torpedoes and not exploding ammunition sank the *Lusitania*, because there was no ammunition aboard. The cover-up was now official.

But there have been critics of these inquiries. One was, of course, the book written by Colin Simpson, who did the research necessary to write his book in the original minutes of the two inquiries.

The Los Angeles Times reviewed Mr. Simpson's book and concluded: "*The Lusitania* proves beyond a reasonable doubt that the British government connived at the sinking of the passenger ship in order to lure America into World War I. The Germans, whose torpedo struck the liner, were the unwitting accomplices or victims of a plot probably concocted by Winston Churchill."

President Wilson was seeking re-election in 1916. He campaigned on his record of "keeping us out of the War" during his first term of office from 1912 to 1916.

Up until America's entry into this war, the American people had followed the wise advice of President George Washington given in his farewell address, delivered to the nation on September 17, 1796. President Washington said: *"It is our true policy to steer clear of permanent alliance with any portion of the foreign world.... Why, by interweaving our destiny with that of any part of Europe, entangle our peace and prosperity in the toils of European ambition, rivalship, interest, humour or caprice?'*

President Washington attempted to warn the American people about getting embroiled in the affairs of Europe. But in 1914, it was not to be. There were those who were secretly planning America's involvement in World War I whether the American people wanted it or not.

The pressure to involve the American government in a European war started in 1909, long before the actual assassination of the, Archduke Franz Ferdinand and his wife on the 28th of June 1914.

Norman Dodd, former director of the Committee to Investigate Tax Exempt Foundations of the U.S. House of Representatives, testified that the Committee was invited to study the minutes of the Carnegie Endowment for International Peace as part of the Committee's investigation. The Committee stated: ***"The trustees of the Foundation brought up a single question. If it is desirable to alter the life of an entire people, is there any means more efficient than war.... They discussed this question... for a year and came up with an answer: There are no known means more efficient than war, assuming the objective is altering the life of an entire people.*** *That leads them to another question: How do we involve the United States in a war. This is in 1909.*

So the decision was made at that time to involve the United States in a war so that the "life of the entire people could be altered." This was the conclusion of a foundation supposedly committed to "peace."

The Zimmerman Telegram 19ᵗʰ January 1917

Zionist Jew Arthur Zimmerman, the German Foreign Secretary sent this telegram to the German ambassador to Mexico, proposing a **Mexican-German alliance in case of war between the United States and Germany, is published on the front pages of newspapers across America. In the telegram, intercepted and deciphered**

by British intelligence, Zimmerman instructed the German ambassador, Count Johann von Bernstorff, to offer significant financial aid to Mexico if it agreed to enter any future US–German conflict as a German ally. If victorious in the conflict, Germany also promised to restore to Mexico, the states of Arizona, New Mexico and Texas.

President Woodrow Wilson learned of the telegram's contents on 26th February; the next day he proposed to Congress that the USA should start arming its ships against possible German attacks. Germany had already aroused Wilson's ire and that of the American public, with its policy of unrestricted submarine warfare and its continued attacks against American ships. Some of those in the United States who still held out for neutrality at first claimed the telegram was a fake. This notion was dispelled two days later, when Zimmerman himself confirmed its authenticity. Public opinion in the United States now swung firmly towards American entrance into World War. On the 2nd April, Wilson went before Congress to deliver a message of war. The United States formally entered the conflict four days later. Zionists had finally set in motion their plan to alter the lives of the entire European population.

A few powerful voices had opposed President Wilson's plea to make war on Germany. Senator Robert La Follette (R–Wisc) said; **"I am speaking of a profession of** democracy that is linked in action with the most brutal and domineering use of autocratic power. Are the people of this country being so well represented in this war movement that we need to go abroad to give other people control of their governments? Will the President and the supporters of this war bill submit it to a vote of the people before the declaration of war goes into effect? Congress is called upon to take, in declaring war upon Germany? Submit the question to the people, you who support it. You who support it dare not do it, for you know that by a vote of more than ten to one the American people as a body would register their declaration against it".

George Norris(R–Neb) was also outraged at the unilateral action taken by the Wilson administration. In a scathing speech he said; **"He had some knowledge about the driving forces behind the call to war. He believed that many Americans had been misled as to the real history and the true facts, by the almost unanimous demand of the great combination of wealth that has a direct financial interest in our participation in the war. Wall Street bankers loaned millions to the Allies, and naturally wanted it repaid. These same forces also held sway in the media. A large number of the great newspapers and news agencies of this country have been controlled and enlisted in the greatest propaganda that the world has ever known,**

to manufacture sentiment in favour of war, and now Congress, urged by the President and backed by the artificial sentiment, is about to declare war and engulf our country in the greatest holocaust that the world has ever known. We are going into war upon the command of gold". And everyone knew who held the gold. Later that same day, the Senate confirmed the declaration of war 82 to 6 and two days thereafter the House concurred, 373 to 50 and three months later American troops were on the ground in Europe, 117465 of them never returned, 204002 would return, most of whom were disabled for life and $22billion was added to the American taxpayer's bill.

WORLD WAR TWO 1939-1945

The Treaty of Versailles which was signed on 28 June 1919 consisting of 440 Articles dictating the terms for Germany's punishment. The treaty was greeted with shock and dismay in Germany and with disbelief in many other countries.

Having won World War1, Woodrow Wilson's Jewish team was anxious to dictate the peace. As it turned out the War would bring benefits to the Zionist cause, in part because of Brandeis' role as a trusted advisor to President Wilson, who was no doubt keenly aware of the finances that Jews had made available to the Allies. The victorious nations convened in Paris in January 1919, and the American Jewish Congress was there as its own delegation. Stephen Wise was in Paris, on assignment from President Wilson to head the Zionist delegation to the peace talks. Many of the delegates were asking how did the, Zionists and Louis Marshall get their own delegation?

The Jewish aim was neither a just implementation of peace, nor fair treatment for Germany, but rather to maximize benefits to the various Jewish communities of Europe and the US. In 1976 Ben Sasson said; "At the beginning of 1919 diplomatic activity in Paris became the main focus of the various attempts to fulfil Jewish aspirations". Fink (1998:n259) concurs: "In March 1919, pro-Zionist and nationalist Jewish delegations arrived in Paris", however "The fervent Zionist Julius Mack and the more moderate Louis Marshall quickly overshadowed the leading American anti-nationalists, Henry Morgenthau, Oscar Straus and Cyrus Alder". It seems all the victorious nations had their own Jewish representatives. Some sought formal and explicit Jewish rights in their own nations and others worked for recognition of a Jewish national state. Emile Dillon, the Irish journalist wrote; **"Of all the collectivities whose interests were furthered at the Conference, the Jews had perhaps the most resourceful and certainly the most influential exponents. There were Jews from Palestine, from Poland, Russia, the Ukraine, Rumania, Greece, Holland, and Belgium; but the largest and most brilliant contingent was sent by the United States".** **It is a fact, he said, "That a considerable number of delegates believed that the real influences behind the Anglo-Saxon people were Semitic".....** **"Henceforth the world will be governed by the Anglo-Saxon people, who, in turn, are swayed by their Jewish elements".**

Among non-Jewish Americans there was a young Herbert Hoover, then secretary of the US Food Administration, and of course, future president. He was accompanied by a Jewish assistant, the financier Lewis Strauss, who remarked on his boss' notable inclination to "champion Jewish rights", especially in Poland. Strauss would later become instrumental in funding early research and development of the atomic bomb.

The brutal and harsh treatment of the Germans at the Conference is well known. They had been promised that the Conference would be a fair settlement of the legitimate war claims of all belligerents, particularly given the complex and convoluted conditions existing at the outbreak of hostilities in 1914. Vis-á-vis, (The Russians threatened Germany, the Germans declare war on Russia, France forms a pact with Russia, Germany declared war on France, Germany entered Belgium, Britain declared war on Germany). As the Conference progressed Wilson and his team decided that Germany alone was responsible for the war and should therefore, bear the full burden of reparations. The impossible conditions forced on Germany set the stage for the rise of National Socialism and the next Great War.

The Rise of National Socialism in Germany

The expeditious rise of Nationalsozialismus (NAZISM) in Germany alarmed and surprised the Anglo-Saxons and the Zionists, what really surprised them most was the fact that they had achieved full employment so soon in spite of the 1929 depression and without assistance or support from external financiers. Nazism was essentially, a traditional barter system far different from capitalism or communism.

Many people were of the opinion that Wall Street and Jewish bankers "financed Hitler." There is documented evidence that Wall Street and Jewish bankers did in fact provide some financial aid for Hitler in the beginning, partly because it appeared to be normal banking practice to do so but mainly to counteract any possible alliance with Stalin. However, when Hitler demonstrated that he could create his own financial system without outside aid the Zionist bankers threatened world war on Germany.

When Hitler was elected Chancellor in 1933 Germany was totally broke. The Treaty of Versaille had imposed unjust and oppressive reparations on the German people, demanding that Germans repay every nation's costs of the war. These costs totalled an estimated three times the value of the entire property of Germany. Cruel currency speculators caused the German mark to devalue to such an extent that it caused the worst runaway inflation in modern times. A sack full of 100 million mark banknotes could not buy a loaf of bread. The national treasury of Germany was empty and homes, farms and commercial properties were bought at ridiculously low prices by speculators and privately owned Jewish banks, while the indigenous German people lived and starved in shacks and sheds.

Never before had inflation of this magnitude occurred which destroyed a nation's currency while confiscating the peoples savings and businesses. This together with onset of the worldwide depression of 1929, the German

Government were at the mercy of mainly Jewish bankers and had to succumb to debt slavery until 1933, when the National Socialists came to power. At this time the German government issued its own currency thereby neutralising international banking cartels' grip on the German economy. The Jews then imposed a boycott on Germany but Hitler initiated an internal credit program and designed a national plan to construct new ports, flood barriers, new roads, canals, the repair of private and public buildings all funded by Germany's own exchequer and bypassed the need of external financial support. Hitler calculated that the cost of his renewal plan was in region of one billion reichsmarks initially called Labour Treasury Certificates. This enabled the Nazis to employ millions of workers paying them with Treasury Certificates. Under the National Socialists, Germany's money wasn't backed by gold (which was owned by the international bankers). It was essentially a receipt for labour and materials delivered to the government. Hitler said, "For every mark issued, we required the equivalent of a mark's worth of work done, or goods produced." The government paid workers in Certificates. Workers used the Certificates to buy other goods and services, thus creating more jobs for more people. In this way the German people climbed out of the crushing debt imposed on them by The Treaty of Versailles together with the international bankers.

Within two years, the unemployment problem had been solved, and Germany was back on its feet. It had a solid, stable currency, with no debt, and no inflation, at a time when millions of people in the United States and other Western countries (controlled by international bankers) were still out of work. Within five years, Germany went from being the poorest nation in Europe to the richest.

Germany even managed to restore foreign trade, despite the international bankers' denial of foreign credit to Germany, and despite the global boycott by Jewish-owned industries. Germany succeeded in this by exchanging equipment and commodities directly with other countries, using a barter system that cut the bankers out of the picture. Germany flourished, since barter eliminates national debt and trade deficits. (Venezuela does the same thing today when it trades oil for commodities, plus medical help, and so on. Hence the bankers are trying to squeeze Venezuela.)

Germany's economic freedom was short-lived; but it left several monuments, including the famous Autobahn, the world's first extensive superhighway. Hjalmar Schacht, a Rothschild agent who was temporarily head of the German central bank, summed it up thus. . . An American banker had commented, "Dr. Schacht, you should come to America. We've lots of money and that's real banking." Schacht replied, "You should come to Berlin. We don't have money. That's real banking." (Schact, the Rothschild agent, actually supported the private international bankers against Germany, and was rewarded by having all charges against him dropped at the Nuremberg trials.)

This economic freedom made Hitler extremely popular with the German people. Germany was rescued from English economic theory, which says that all currency must be borrowed against the gold owned by a private and secretive banking cartel ~ such as the Federal Reserve, or the Central Bank of Europe ~ rather than issued by the government for the benefit of the people.

Canadian researcher Dr. Henry Makow (who is Jewish himself) says the main reason why the bankers arranged for a world war against Germany was that Hitler sidestepped the bankers by creating his own money, thereby freeing the German people. Worse, this freedom and prosperity threatened to spread to other nations. Hitler had to be stopped!

Makow quotes from the 1938 interrogation of C. G. Rakovsky, one of the founders of Soviet Bolsevism and a Trotsky intimate. Rakovsky was tried in show trials in the USSR under Stalin. According to Rakovsky, Hitler was at first funded by the international bankers, through the bankers' agent Hjalmar Schacht. The bankers financed Hitler in order to control Stalin, who had usurped power from their agent Trotsky. Then Hitler became an even bigger threat than Stalin when Hitler started printing his own money. (Stalin came to power in 1922 which was eleven years before Hitler came to power.) **Rakovsky said: "Hitler took over the privilege of manufacturing money, and not only physical**

moneys, but also financial ones. He took over the machinery of falsification and put it to work for the benefit of the people. Can you possibly imagine what would have come if this had infected a number of other states?"

(Henry Makow, "Hitler Did Not Want War" www. savethemales.com March 21, 2004).

'In Billions for the Bankers, Debts for the People (1984)', Sheldon Emry commented: "Germany issued debt-free and interest-free money from 1935, on which accounts for Germany's startling rise from the depression to a world power in five years. The German government financed its entire operations from 1935 to 1945 without gold, and without debt. It took the entire Capitalist and Communist world to destroy the German revolution, and bring Europe back under the heel of the Bankers."

These facts do not appear in any textbooks today, since Jews own most publishing companies. What does appear is the disastrous runaway inflation suffered in 1923 by the Weimar Republic, which governed Germany from 1919 to 1933. Today's textbooks use this inflation to twist truth into its opposite. They cite the radical devaluation of the German mark as an example of what happens when governments print their own money, rather than borrow it from private cartels.

In reality, the Weimar financial crisis began with the impossible reparations payments imposed at the Treaty of Versailles. Hjalmar Schacht - the Rothschild agent who was currency commissioner for the Republic opposed letting the German government print its own money." The Treaty of Versailles is a model of ingenious measures for the economic destruction of Germany. Germany could not find any way of holding its head above the water, other than by this inflationary expedient of printing bank notes."

Schact echoes the textbook lie -that Weimar inflation was caused when the German government printed its own money. However, in his 1967 book The Magic of Money, Schact let the cat out of the bag by revealing that it was the PRIVATELY-OWNED Reichsbank, not the German government that was pumping new currency into the economy. Thus, the PRIVATE BANK caused the Weimar hyper-inflation.

Like the U.S. Federal Reserve, the Reichsbank was overseen by appointed government officials, but was operated for private gain. What drove the wartime inflation into hyperinflation was speculation by foreign investors, who sold the mark short, betting on its decreasing value. In the manipulative device known as the short sale, speculators borrow something they don't own, sell it, and then "cover" by buying it back at the lower price. Speculation in the German mark was made possible because the privately owned Reichsbank (not yet under Nazi control) made massive amounts of currency available for borrowing. This currency, like U.S. currency today, was created with accounting entries on the bank's books. Then the funny-money was lent at compound interest. When the Reichsbank could not keep up with the voracious demand for marks, other private banks were allowed to create marks out of nothing, and to lend them at interest. The result was runaway debt and inflation.

Thus, according to Schacht himself, the German government did not cause the Weimar hyperinflation. On the contrary, the government (under the National Socialists) got hyperinflation under control. The National Socialists put the Reichsbank under strict government regulation, and took prompt corrective measures to eliminate foreign speculation. One of those measures was to eliminate easy access to funny-money loans from private banks. Then Hitler got Germany back on its feet by having the public government, issue Treasury Certificates.

Schacht, the Rotchschild agent, disapproved of this government fiat money, and wound up getting fired as head of the Reichsbank when he refused to issue it. Nonetheless, he acknowledged in his later memoirs that allowing the government to issue the money it needed did not produce the price inflation predicted by classical economic theory, which says that currency must be borrowed from private cartels.

What causes hyper-inflation is uncontrolled speculation. When speculation is coupled with debt (owed to private banking cartels) the result is disaster. On the other hand, when a government issues currency in carefully measured ways, it causes supply and demand to increase together, leaving prices unaffected. Hence there is no inflation, no debt, no unemployment, and no need for income taxes.

Naturally this terrifies the private bankers, since it eliminates their powers. It also terrifies Jews, since their control of banking allows them to buy the media, the government, and everything else. Therefore, to those who delight in saying "Jews financed Hitler," I ask that they please look at all the facts. "Permit me to issue and control the money of a nation, and I care not who makes its laws." - Mayer Amschel Rothschild, [quoted in Money Creators (1935) by Gertrude Coogan, p. 329]

> "Debt, particularly international debt, is the first and over-mastering grip. Through it men in high places are suborned and alien powers and influences are introduced into the body politic. When the debt grip has been firmly established, control of every form of publicity and political activity soon follows, together with a full grip on industrialists."
>
> - Archibald Maule Ramsay,
> The Nameless War (1952)

"History, as seen by a Monetary Economist, is a continuous struggle between producers and non-producers, and those who try to make a living by inserting a false system of book-keeping between the producers and their just recompense . . . The usurers act through fraud, falsification, superstitions, habits and, when these methods do not function, they let loose a war. Everything hinges on monopoly, and the particular monopolies hinge around the great illusionistic monetary monopoly." - Ezra Pound, "An Introduction to the Economic Nature of the United States" (1950)

"Rothschild's ill-gotten wealth also effectively bought his family the first Jewish seat in the British Parliament and even membership in the British aristocracy. By combining the power of their own family's huge banks and other Jewish-owned banks, they could literally bring a nation's economy to its knees. By dominating international banking, they could set their own financial terms to cash-hungry nations and amass even greater riches. Because of the competitive advantages of Rothschild's international contacts, Jews dominated private banking throughout Europe. For instance, there was almost a complete absence of Gentile banking firms in Prussia in the late 19th century. In 1923 Berlin there were 150 Jewish banks and only 11 non- Jewish banks. In the stock market, schemes similar to Rothschild's Waterloo ploy have been used for generations, finally resulting in the center of world trading, Wall Street, becoming dominated by Jewish stock and investment- banker operations." - David Duke, Jewish Supremacism (2002)

"One of these means is concentrated in the world of finance. It has not been primarily a matter of manifesting a genius for making money or for actually amassing it in colossal amounts, though of course this of itself has weighed heavily. But primarily it has been a matter of setting up a money system, which the entire economic life of each nation was dependent upon, and which developed a power so vast and irresistible that it placed itself beyond all effective governmental interference, and thereby became in fact a power above government, a power that could bring even governments to their knees." - William G. Simpson, Which Way Western Man? (1977)

"Thus arose, the school of international finance, in which the Rothschilds and other Jewish money-lenders were very able teachers. In fact the mentality of England was developing in such a direction as to enable the Jews to prepare for the blessed day when Britain would be one of their colonies. These three principles — ruthless competition, free trade at any cost, and the investment of money without any regard to blood, nation, or race are fundamental to the international capitalism in the interests of which Britain has mobilized her forces to destroy National-Socialist Germany. They are the basic axioms of the old order".

William Joyce, Twilight
Over England (1940)

"The notion that the level of production should be controlled by monetary considerations belongs to a very primitive and superstitious stage of social evolution. Indeed, there are few savage tribes that would accept it as it is accepted in Britain today. Suppose that in some very backward island, a shell standard of money prevailed. Assume also that some malicious or half-witted creature managed to acquire half the shells in the island and to drop them into the water beyond recovery. The chiefs and witch-doctors would have to hold a council of emergency. But if the rulers of that island decreed that because half the money of the community **had** been lost, hunting and fishing and tilling must now be reduced by fifty per cent, there would be a hot time in the old town that night. In such a simple state of society, the criminal absurdity of the proposal would be obvious to the meanest and most untutored intellect. Yet a policy which the most undeveloped savage tribe would reject as nonsense has been accepted by the British people as a sacred ritual for many years. Thus, of course, international finance, by restricting supplies and causing shortage, can produce whatever conditions of marketing that may be most profitable to its self. If there is one truth against which the Old School of Finance is fighting today, it is the supreme verity that production of goods should be based on the needs of the people, the only limit being the limit of natural resources and raw materials. Since the dawn of human history, the great struggle of man has been to wrest from Nature by force and cunning the means of life and enjoyment. It was only when the blessings of modern democracy made their appearance one hundred and fifty years ago, that he was told, in an arbitrary manner, that his efforts must be slackened and regulated henceforth by the private interests of an infinitesimal proportion of the world's population." - William Joyce, Twilight Over England (1940)

"Some people think Federal Reserve Banks are United States Government institutions. They are not Government institutions. They are private credit monopolies which prey upon the people of the United States for the benefits of themselves and their foreign customers; foreign and domestic speculators and swindlers; and rich and predatory money lenders. In that dark crew of financial pirates there are those who would cut a man's throat to get a dollar out of his pocket; there are those who send money into states to buy votes to control our legislation; and there are those that maintain an international propaganda for deceiving us... that will permit them to cover up their past misdeeds and set again in motion their gigantic train of crime . . . Mr. Chairman, we have in this country one of the most corrupt institutions the world has ever known. The Federal Reserve Board has cheated the United States out of enough money to pay the national debt... Mr. Speaker, it is a monstrous thing for this great Nation to have its destiny presided over by a treasonous system acting in secret concert with International pirates and usurers. Every effort has been made by the FED to conceal its power. But the truth is the FED has usurped the government of the United States. It controls everything here. It controls foreign relations. It makes and breaks governments at will". Congressman Louis T. McFadden, Speech on Floor of the House of Representatives, 1934

> Dr. Frederick Soddy's book
> 'Wealth, Virtual Wealth &
> Debt (1926)' states that;

"Our money system is nothing better than a confidence trick, the "money power" which has been able to overshadow ostensibly responsible government is not the power of the merely ultra -rich but is nothing more or less than a new technique to destroy money by adding and withdrawing figures in bank ledgers, without the slightest concern for the interests of the community or the real role money ought to perform therein ... to allow it to become a source of revenue to private issuer's is to create, first, a secret and illicit arm of government and, last, a rival power strong enough to ultimately overthrow all other forms of government.".

"A great industrial nation is controlled by its system of credit. Our system of credit is concentrated. The growth of the nation, therefore, and all of our activities are in the hands of a few men. We have become one of the worst ruled, one of the most completely controlled and dominated governments in the civilized world ... no longer a government of free opinion ... but a government by the opinion and duress of small groups of domineering me".

President Woodrow Wilson,
The New Freedom (1913)

"JEWS have no religious scruples regarding money where gentiles are concerned. They now have the means to carry out their war of annihilation of the West. They would not surface as a fighting unit and openly attack their hated enemy. They remained invisible. Their strategy was to organize the entire Jewish People into a Fifth Column whose purpose is to penetrate the West and destroy everything. This is being accomplished by exacerbating natural disputes between the Western States and influencing the results in favour of Liberalism as opposed to Authority; that is, materialism, free trade and usury, as opposed to Western Socialism; Internationalism as opposed to Western unity. MONEY was their sword and buckler. Hate and revenge their motif."

James von Brunn, "Kill the Best Gentiles! (2009).

"Though the British public was kept in total ignorance as to the true significance of what was taking place in Spain, two countries in Europe were alive to the situation. Germany and Italy had each in their turn experienced the throes of communist revolution, and emerged victorious over this foulest of earthly plagues. They knew who had financed and organised the International Brigades; and with what foul purpose Barcelona had been declared in October 1936 the Capital of the Soviet States of Western Europe. At the critical moment they intervened in just sufficient strength to counter the International Brigade, and enable the Spanish people to organise their own army, which, in due course, easily settled the matter. That settled the matter, that is to say, as far as Spain was concerned. There was, however, another settlement to come. International Jewry had been seriously thwarted. They would not rest henceforward until they could have their revenge; until they could by hook or crook turn the guns of the rest of the world against these two States, which in addition to thwarting their designs in Spain were in the process of placing Europe upon a system independent of gold and usury, which, if permitted to develop, would break the Jewish power forever."

Archibald Maule Ramsay,
The Nameless War (1952

The Path to War

The remaining points become clear, simply by stepping through some key events and observations as they happened chronologically:

As is well known, Jews worldwide confronted Hitler as soon as he assumed power in 1933—witness the infamous "Judea Declares War on Germany" headline in the UK's *Daily Express* of 24 March 1933. In a sense, this was understandable. Putting an end to a post-World War I Weimar Republic dominated by Jews, Hitler quickly banished them from positions of power, and placed immediate restrictions on the movement and business activities of Freemasons and Jews. In fact, one may speculate that this was not unrelated to Germany's amazing economic renaissance.

But the Zionist controlled Western media did not see it that way. As early as April 1933, the *New York Times* was reporting on the "economic extermination of Jews in Germany" (April 6). Two months later we read, simply, that "Hitler's program is one of extermination" (June 29). In August, we are shocked to learn that "600,000 Jews are facing certain extinction" (August 16). Here we can graphically see how the 'extermination' myth rapidly evolved, from a plan of economic exclusion.

For the Germans, Western (particularly American) media meant *Jewish* media. As early as 1934, they viewed it as a potential threat. A communiqué by the German ambassador to the US, Hans Luther, observed that America possessed "the strongest Jewish propaganda machine in the world." This comment was made in light of Jewish dominance in Hollywood, and the fact that Jews owned two of the major American newspapers, the *New York Times* and the *Washington Post*. Luther's impression was held by the German leadership throughout the war. Goebbels, for example, wrote the following in his diary entry of

24 April 1942: "Some statistics are given to me on the proportion of Jews in American radio, film, and press. The percentage is truly frightening. Jewry controls 100% of the film business, and between 90 and 95% of press and radio.

By the mid-1930s, Germany was in the midst of their astounding economic recovery, one that was particularly striking given their ruination after World War I and that it occurred during the Great Depression. Within just his first four years, Hitler had reduced unemployment from 6 million to 1 million; the jobless rate fell from 43.8% when he took office, to effectively *zero* by the end of 1938. In just four years, he increased GNP by 37%, and oversaw a 400% increase in auto production. In effect, he single-handedly ended the Depression in Germany. Two more years, and the nation would be a world power of the first rank. The success of the Nazi economy was based on monasticism.

Germany thus emerged as a viable competitor to the traditional global powers. Churchill felt particularly threatened. In a congressional testimony, US General Robert Wood recalled a statement by Churchill from 1936: "Germany is getting too strong. We must smash her." This suggests a belligerence on Churchill's part long before any aggressions by Hitler. It is important to remember, it was the UK that declared war on Germany, not vice versa.

In October 1937, Roosevelt gave his famous 'quarantine' speech. Here we find one of the first indications, albeit indirect, that he anticipates a time when the US would come into direct conflict with Germany, and his prophecy that the public would favour such a war. The danger of Hitler is exaggerated; neutrality and isolation are disparaged; baseless assertions and cautiously conditional statements are thrown out—and all in the language of peace. Should Hitler prevail, "let no one imagine that America will escape, that this Western Hemisphere will not be attacked." "There is no escape through mere isolation or neutrality," he said; "international anarchy destroys every foundation for peace." "We are determined to keep out of war," said FDR, "yet we cannot insure ourselves against the disastrous effects of war and the dangers of involvement." Sparing no hyperbole, he added that, if Germany initiates a war, "the storm will rage till every flower of culture is trampled and all human beings are levelled in a vast chaos." This is difficult to read except as an indication that the path of violent confrontation had already been decided upon, and that the long process had begun to persuade a reluctant public that they must support it.

By this time, Jewish lobbies around the world, but especially in the UK and US, began to press hard for military action, to intervene on behalf of their beleaguered coreligionists in Nazi Germany, and to once again overthrow a hated regime—never mind that the Germans may have had some right to self-determination. One of the first clear pieces of evidence of this came in early 1938, from the Polish ambassador to the US, Jerzy Potocki. He reported back to Warsaw on his observations of the American political scene:

> *The pressure of the Jews on President Roosevelt and on the State Department is becoming ever more powerful... The Jews are right now the leaders in creating a war psychosis which would plunge the entire world into war and bring about general catastrophe. This mood is becoming more and more apparent. In their definition of democratic states, the Jews have also created real chaos; they have mixed together the idea of democracy and communism, and have above all raised the banner of burning hatred against Nazism.*

> *This hatred has become a frenzy. It is propagated everywhere and by every means: in theatres, in the cinema, and in the press. The Germans are portrayed as a nation living under the arrogance of Hitler which wants to conquer the whole world and drown all of humanity in an ocean of blood. In conversations with Jewish press representatives, I have repeatedly come up against the inexorable and convinced view that war is inevitable. This international Jewry exploits every means of propaganda to oppose any tendency towards any kind of consolidation and understanding between nations. In this way, the conviction is growing*

steadily but surely in public opinion here that the Germans and their satellites, in the form of fascism, are enemies who must be subdued by the 'democratic world.

Such a view is confirmed in a letter by Senator Hiram Johnson (R-Cal.), written to his son that same year. The pro- and anti-war camps were clear: "all the Jews [are] on one side, wildly enthusiastic for the President, and willing to fight to the last American." Though sympathetic, Johnson had no interest in fighting a war on their behalf. He and other like-minded politicians wanted to speak out, "but everybody is afraid—I confess, I shrink from it—of offending the Jews." The situation has hardly changed in 75 years.

For his part, Bernie Baruch was certainly itching for a fight. Speaking to General George Marshall, he said "We are going to lick that fellow Hitler. He isn't going to get away with it." One wonders how he would know this, in 1938. Actually, it's not much of a mystery: Churchill apparently told him so. As Sherwood (1948: 111) recounts, Churchill— then still First Lord of the Admiralty—said this to Baruch: "War is coming very soon. We will be in it and you (the United States) will be in it. You (Baruch) will be running the show over there, but I will be on the side-lines over here." This is an astonishing claim; how would Churchill know such a thing, in 1938? The *Anschluss* with Austria had been completed in March that year, and Germany annexed the Sudetenland in October, but the Munich Accord was signed in September, nominally preserving a kind of tenuous peace. So what could have convinced Churchill that war was inevitable, and that the Americans would be running the show? *Kristallnacht*, perhaps? Was that the last straw, for the global Jewish lobby?

Apparently Lord Beaverbrook thought so. Writing to Frank Gannett in December 1938, he made this striking statement:

> *The Jews are after [Prime Minister] Chamberlain. He is being terribly harassed by them... All the Jews are against him... They have got a big position in the press here [in the UK]... I am shaken. The Jews may drive us into war [and] their political influence is moving us in that direction. (cited in Nasaw 2012: 357-358)*

Beaverbrook was a prominent and influential media executive and politician, rather like the Rupert Murdoch of his day. He was well positioned to make such a claim.

The year 1939 opened with FDR's State of the Union speech—and more veiled threats. "We have learned that God-fearing democracies of the world...cannot safely be indifferent to international lawlessness anywhere. They cannot forever let pass, without effective protest, acts of aggression against sister nations." He consequently called for an unprecedented peacetime allocation of $2 billion for national defence. This was a message to Hitler and to all those Americans who might oppose intervention in European affairs.

Media Blitz

Jewish-run media was becoming very active by this time. The newspapers, for example, had found much disagreement with Washington on domestic issues, but "Roosevelt's standing with the press on foreign policy matters was much stronger," according to Cole (1983: 478). Apart from the *Chicago Tribune* and the Hearst papers, most dailies backed intervention. Unsurprisingly, "the more prestigious and influential news publications strongly supported the president." These included the *New York Times*, the *New York Herald Tribune*, the *Chicago Daily News*, and *Time Magazine*.

The motion picture industry certainly did its part to get America into war. Given that it took at least a year to get a motion picture from conception to theatre, and that efforts to produce pro-war films did not start in earnest until 1937, it was well into 1939 before they began to appear. Early efforts like *Confessions of a Nazi Spy* and *Beasts of Berlin* came out that year, and set the stage for a flood of films over the next three years. In 1940, Hollywood released graphic and high-impact films like Escape and Mortal Storm; Hitchcock's *Foreign Correspondent* came out that year, as did Chaplin's *The Great Dictator*. In May, two major studio heads, Jack and Harry Warner—more accurately known as Itzhak and Hirsz Wonskolaser—wrote to Roosevelt, assuring him that they would "do all in our power within the motion picture industry...to show the

American people the worthiness of the cause for which the free peoples of Europe are making such tremendous sacrifices". The public were expected to appreciate such unselfish, high-minded public service amongst corporate executives.

On 19 August 1941, Churchill told his war cabinet that Roosevelt was doing all he could to provoke an attack by the Axis powers. (This information only came to light in 1972). *"[Roosevelt] was obviously determined that they [the US] should come in. ... The president said to me that he would wage war but not declare it, and that he would become more and more provocative. If the Germans did not like it, they could attack American forces. ... Everything was being done to force an 'incident.' The president has made it clear that he would look for an 'incident' which could justify him in opening hostilities"*

The Japanese attack on Pearl Harbour provided the justification Roosevelt needed.

Pearl Harbour memo shows US warned of Japanese attack

On the 7th December 1941 the Japanese attacked Pearl Harbour and slaughtered 2459 and injured 1282 US troops and virtually wiped out the US Pacific fleet. That day was described by President Franklin D. Roosevelt as "a date that will live in infamy". On the 70th anniversary of Japan's devastating attack on the US Pacific Fleet at Pearl Harbour, Hawaii, new evidence has been discovered which shows that President Franklin D. Roosevelt had been warned three days before the attack that the Japanese empire was planning to bombard Hawaii with a view to "open conflict". The details are contained in a declassified memorandum from the Office of Naval Intelligence. "In anticipation of possible open conflict with this country, Japan is vigorously utilizing every available agency to secure military, naval and commercial information, paying particular attention to the West Coast, the Panama Canal and the Territory of Hawaii," Dated December 4, 1941, marked as confidential, and entitled "Japanese intelligence and propaganda in the United States," it gives an account of Japan's surveillance of Hawaii under a section headlined "Methods of Operation and Points of Attack."

It seems Washington deliberately ignored the warning in the hope that Japanese would cause an incidence and justify a declaration of war on the Axis.

Roosevelt declared war on Japan the day after the blitz on Pearl Harbour. Japan, Germany and Italy reciprocated with their own declarations, but America's involvement in the war turned the tide against the Axis powers and ultimately led the Allies to victory.

Americans, who a year previously had been assured by Roosevelt that they would not be sent to fight foreign wars, suddenly found their fates transformed. The US military swelled, with 16 million heading off to war. The War Powers Act gave the president supreme executive authority. The "America First" movement, which had lobbied against the country's entry into the war and at its peak, had 800,000 members, disbanded within days.

ROALD DAHL, PALESTINE 1941

Roald Dahl, in his book 'Going Solo' describes how he discovered a landing strip in a field of corn near Mount Carmel in Palestine which had been built by a German Jewish man who was managing an orphanage for Jewish refugees. "I made a landing, pulled up and switched off the engine. A stream of children surrounded my Hurricane, there must have been forty or fifty of them. Then out came a tall bearded man who ordered them to stand away from the plane. 'Welcome to our little settlement' he said, speaking with a strong German accent speaking like a parody of Hitler. "So where do you go from here?" "We don't go anywhere", he said, "We stay here". "Then you will all become Palestinians or perhaps you are already". He said, "No, I do not think we will become Palestinians". "Then what will you do?" I asked. "You are a young man who is flying aeroplanes and I do not expect you to understand our problems". "Don't you care whether we beat Hitler or not"? I asked him. "Of course I care. It is essential that Hitler be defeated. But that is only a matter of months and years. Historically it will be a very short battle. My battle is one that has been going on since the time of Christ, we need a homeland; we need a country of our own, even the Zulus have Zululand but we have nothing". "If you want something badly enough", he said, "and if you need something badly enough, you can always get it."

Roald Dahl had stumbled on a typical Zionist settlement which was part of their on-going plan since the 1890s to insidiously occupy Palestine and turn it into a Jewish State. Towards the beginning of the 20th century the Zionists had developed a policy to covertly purchase Palestinian properties, for the formation of Jewish communities and bases that would accommodate their military when the time was right to announce the formation of the State of Israel.

> *'The failure of the Russian Revolution 1905 and the wave of pogroms and repressions that followed caused growing numbers of Russian Jewish youth to emigrate to Palestine as pioneer settlers. By 1914 there were about 90,000 Jews in Palestine; 13,000 settlers lived in 43 Jewish agricultural settlements, many of them supported by the French Jewish philanthropist Baron Edmond de Rothschild'.*
> **Zionism: Ency. Britannica.**

In 1941 the Zionists set up a military unit of crypto Israeli soldiers known as Mustta'ribeen or mista'arvim in Hebrew, to infiltrate the Arab nations in the Middle-East by disguising themselves as Arabs. The agents were given rigorous training and taught to think and act like Arabs. This unit was part of the Palmach (Hebrew, Strike Force), an elite division of the Haganah (Hebrew, Defence) militia, which later formed the core of the Israeli army. Haganah, initially disguised as a labour organisation representing Jews in Palestine from 1920 to 1948. Its aim was to defend the Palestine Jewish community if the British army were to retreat from Palestine, Jewish settlements might come under attack from the Arab population. In June 1941 mixed squads of Palmach and Australians began operating in Lebanon and Syria. The success of these operations led British GHQ to fund a sabotage training camp for three hundred men at Mishmar HaEmek. When the British ordered the dismantling of the Palmach after the Allied victory at the Second Battle of El Alamein in 1942, the organisation went underground and they did not go away.

Israel's perceived need for a secret service was fulfilled by Avraham Stern who had formed the Stern Gang aka Lehi whose avowed aim was to evict the British from Palestine by force, to allow unrestricted immigration of Jews and the formation of a Jewish state, a new totalitarian Hebrew Republic. Walter Edward Guinness 1st Baron Moyne, DSO & Bar, PC was an Anglo Irish politician and businessman. He served as the British minister of state in the Middle East until he was assassinated in Egypt by the Jewish terrorist group Lehi 6th November 1944. The assassination of Lord Moyne sent shock waves through Palestine and the rest of the world. Mr W. Churchill who once described himself as a Zionist told the House of Commons: "If our dreams for Zionism are to end in the smoke of assassins' pistols and our labours for its future to produce only a new set of gangsters worthy of Nazi Germany, many like myself will have to reconsider the position we have maintained so constantly and so long in the past. If there is to be any hope of a peaceful and successful future for Zionism, these wicket activities must cease, and those responsible for them must be destroyed root and branch."

The Jewish community wholeheartedly condemned the assassination of Lord Moyne. The assassins were arrested, tried and executed by the Egyptians and their bodies exchanged for twenty Egyptian prisoners held by Israel. Later, the Israelis gave the assassins a state funeral. **Wikipedia: Lehi and Palmach**

The Hiram Key Revisited

The Masonic ritual tells how King Solomon decided to inaugurate a new priestly order based upon the mysteries and rites of the Enochian priesthood. And it appears that their mission was nothing less than to bring about a new world order. This we deduce was to be a world where all gods were viewed as part of the same. Quite simply it appears that Solomon invented the modern concept of monotheism – an all-embracing godhead, based on Yahweh as one supreme force, an amalgamation of every interpretation of the creative force. This new supreme deity is the god of modern Judaism, Christianity and Islam.

The members of Solomon's priestly order were to be in possession of secrets that would be passed on from father to son. The priesthood was to be unseen by the common man. Their mission was to build a world in which they would use their influence to ensure that all gods were honoured to the glory of the ultimate godhead. Their task was to unify the entire world in a single peaceful and tolerant society where god ruled through the king, his regent on Earth. They were to achieve their objective by any means, including the judicious use of money, political influence and if all else fails, force.

Naturally, the centre of this new great order was to be Jerusalem.

These Enochian priests were to become a hereditary priesthood that would carry their ancient knowledge down the generations. And as we will demonstrate, 2500 years later this priesthood would continue its works under the guise of an order called Freemasonry.

The Hiram Key Revisited: Freemasonry: a Plan for a New World Order Paperback – January 1, 1999 **by <u>Christopher Knight</u> (Author), <u>Alan Butler</u> (Author)**

"**The Great Revolt**", was a nationalist uprising by Palestinian Arabs against the British administration of the 'Palestine Mandate', a demand for Arab independence and the end of the policy of open-ended Jewish immigration and land purchases with the stated goal of establishing a "Jewish National Home". In spite of intense Arab opposition, the Masonic State of Israel was founded on the 14th May 1948 and was immediately recognized and supported, by the Masonic United States and the Masonic United Kingdom. Israeli propaganda at that time portrayed the new state as being, a benign, kindly and accommodating towards the Muslim and Christian Arabs who were the majority of the citizens of Palestine. However, Israeli persecution of the Arabs continued soon after the formation of the new state, causing the deaths of more than 46,000 Muslims and Christian, Arabs since 1947.

Ján Ludvík Hyman Binyamin Hoch.
Aka Ian Robert Maxwell

He was a member of a poor Jewish family in Czechoslovakia. During WWII he served in the British Army where he attained the rank of captain and was awarded the Military Cross in 1945. He was attached to the Foreign Office in Berlin where he served for two years. Maxwell naturalised as a British subject in 1946 and changed his name by deed poll in June 1948 and finalised a deal with Czechoslovakia to arm Israel in the 1948 Arab-Israeli War. Czech military assistance was crucial for the Zionists to establish the State of Israel and it was Maxwell's covert help in smuggling aircraft parts into Palestine that gave the Israelis air-supremacy during their 1948 war against the Arabs. Maxwell became a media mogul which enabled him to support the State of Israel's propaganda department. Shortly before Maxwell's death,

Ari Ben-Menashe a former employee of Israel's Military Intelligence Directorate alleged that Maxwell was a Mossad agent. Following Maxwell's mysterious death he was given a state funeral by Israel before he was buried on the Mount of Olives in Jerusalem. Maxwell had investments estimated at £300,000,000 in Israel. Maxwell's association and support for the Zionists is typical of the international Jewry, whose generosity knows no bounds when investing in the development of the State of Israel, their financial support has enabled it to become one the world's biggest producers and exporters of arms and military hardware, together with a wide range of industrial items. Jews know that war is the only market open to producers of military hardware. Knowing that Israel has a reported 80 nuclear war-heads and a quantity of chemical weapons, is a great worry to the civilized world, as the Jews have a psychic relationship with the ancient Jews of Masada. **Wikipedia: Robert Maxwell.**

Korean War 1950-1953

United States involvement in the Korean War was due to the onset of communism in the Asian nations. The Capitalist nations led by the USA foresaw the demise of the capital financial system and the consequential loss of power over their populations if communist monetary philosophy was to become widespread. It had to be stopped in order to save the great western banking companies. By 1953 the Korean War had become a stalemate but the advocators of communism had lost many of their supporters and the West developed new financial programs and banking systems to further consolidate their dominance of the international money markets. The cost of the Korean War: 36,516 Americans killed, 92,134 wounded and a €67billion bill for the tax payers. The total number of casualties and costs for all the other countries involved in this war was proportionally similar.

Julius and Ethel Rosenberg

Julius and **Ethel Rosenberg** were members of a Jewish family who were American citizens, that spied with others, for the Soviet Union, they were tried, convicted, and executed by the federal government of the United States. They provided top-secret information about radar, sonar, and jet propulsion engines to the USSR and were accused of transmitting valuable nuclear weapon designs to the Soviet Union; at that time the United States was the only country in the world with nuclear weapons.

Other convicted co-conspirators were imprisoned, including Ethel's brother, David Greenglass, who supplied documents from Los Alamos to Julius and who served 10 years of a 15-year sentence; Harry Gold, who identified Greenglass and served 15 years in federal prison as the courier for Greenglass. Klaus Fuchs, a German scientist working in Los Alamos and handled by Gold, provided vastly more important information to the Soviets. He was convicted in Great Britain and served nine years and four months in prison

In 2014, five historians who had published works based on the Rosenberg case wrote that Soviet documents show that Ethel Rosenberg hid money and espionage paraphernalia for Julius, served as an intermediary for communications with his Soviet intelligence contacts, relayed her personal evaluation of individuals whom Julius considered recruiting, and was present at meetings with his sources. They also demonstrate that Julius reported to the KGB how Ethel persuaded Ruth Greenglass to travel to New Mexico to recruit David Greenglass as a spy. On April 4, 1951 – Judge Kaufman settled into his courtroom chair, turned to Julius and Ethel Rosenberg and sentenced them to death. They were traitors, he explained, guilty of "putting into the hands of the Russians the A-bomb years before our best scientists predicted Russia would perfect the bomb." And by empowering the Soviets they had caused Communist aggression in Korea – where American casualties topped 50,000 and increased daily.

Vietnam War 1955-1975

The Gulf of Tonkin. Questions about the Gulf of Tonkin incidents have persisted for more than 40 years. But once-classified documents and tapes released in the past several years, combined with previously uncovered facts, clarifies that high government officials distorted facts and deceived the American public, extensively aided by the Jewish Media about the so-called events that led to full U.S. involvement in the Vietnam War in which 58,209 Americans were killed and 153,303 wounded, 23214 disabled, more than 70,000 suicides and cost more than €900 billion.

THE SUEZ CRISIS AND THE PROTOCOL OF SÉVRES 1956

On 24 October 1956, in a private villa in Sèvres on the outskirts of Paris, representatives of the British, French, and Israeli governments, at the end of a three-day meeting which was concealed behind a thick veil of secrecy, signed a most curious document which later came to be known as the Protocol of Sèvres. The document set out in precise detail the plan of the three governments to attack Egypt. The plan, in a nutshell, was that Israel would attack the Egyptian army near the Suez Canal, and that this attack would serve as the pretext for an Anglo-French military intervention. Written in French and typed in three copies, this Protocol was signed by Patrick Dean, an Assistant Under-Secretary at the Foreign Office for Britain, by foreign minister Christian Pineau for France, and by prime minister David Ben-Gurion for Israel.

The senior members of the Israeli delegation to the talks in Paris were David Ben-Gurion, who was defence minister as well as prime minister, Moshe Dayan, the IDF chief of staff, and Shimon Peres, the director-general of the ministry of defence.

Israel invades Egypt; Suez Crisis begins.

On October 29th 1956 Israeli armed forces push into Egypt toward the Suez Canal, initiating the Suez Crisis. They would soon be joined by French and British forces, creating a serious Cold War problem in the Middle East. Casualties resulting from 'The Suez Crisis', is estimated to be more than **3000** with Egypt reporting the highest number. British recorded **16** deaths and **96** wounded while French casualties included ten dead and **33** wounded. Israeli casualties were 172 dead and 817 wounded.

THE IRISH IN THE AMERICAN WAR OF INDEPENDENCE

It is estimated that Irish volunteers made up fifty-percent of Washington's Continental Army. It is further estimated that educated Irish Presbyterians and Dissenting Protestants aka; (Scotch-Irish) formed a large part of the officer corps they were steeped in Freemasonry and fully aware that they were engaged in the establishment of a Masonic State. The uneducated Irish Catholic contingent formed many battalions of foot-soldiers, they were oblivious to the Freemason's real objective and believed they were fighting for multiple freedoms in defeating the 'Old Enemy' the English Establishment. Following the British surrender at Yorktown and the establishment of the American Republic, the Scotch-Irish were awarded plum positions in the new administration and the Irish Catholics found themselves in a different frying pan, condemned to traditional 'pick and shovel' work, because they were Catholics and Jesus Christ was an anathema to both Jews and Masons. Discrimination and bigotry against Catholics was very much in evidence, and neither did the Scotch-Irish have any mercy for their Catholic countrymen in the USA. Prejudice towards Catholics has continued unabated to present day, Jewish-Masonic efforts to finally destroy Catholicism has intensified in recent years on all fronts. Since the foundation of the USA more than twenty presidents have been of Irish Protestant decent, which confirms Irish Protestants have been totally integrated into American Freemasonry so successfully that they managed to put twenty of their men into the White House. JF Kennedy was the first and only Catholic president and his election was obviously unforeseen and therefore invalid, his presence in the Oval Office was sacrilegious from a masonic point of view and a marksman used a **'magic bullet'** to save the Zionist-Masonic State, safely installing a masonic brother, L.B. Johnson in the White House. Johnson appointed two Masonic brothers, Edgar Hoover to research and Judge Warren to chair, a commission to investigate what really happened at the Dealey Plaza in Dallas. They mysteriously concluded that one **Magic Bullet** killed J.F. Kennedy and seriously injured Texas Governor John Connally? Following the publication of the Warren Commission's findings, the Zionist-masonic media went into over-drive supporting absolutely the absurd conclusions of Warren's commission. Anyone who voiced opposition to Warren was immediately stereotyped as a conspiracy-theorist who should be ignored. It was not long before the Zionist-mason media set about destroying JF Kennedy's image world-wide by inventing and publishing a series of sordid fictitious relationships, portraying him as a super-stud in spite of the fact that he suffered from congenital spine problems and Addison's disease, together with other disabilities. There are no records of him sexually abusing anyone, if there were, the media would have published each and every detail. Kennedy's enemies were not content just to assassinate him, they also needed to destroy his image, his legacy and his policies:-

It is remarkable that Lee Harvey's assassin was a Jewish man called Jack Ruby who had a shady history. **Ruby died** of a pulmonary embolism, on January 3, 1967, at Parkland Hospital, Dallas, Texas.

> **"For we are opposed around the world by a monolithic and ruthless conspiracy, that relies on covert means for expanding its sphere of influence on infiltration instead of invasion, on subversion instead of elections, on intimidation instead of choice, on guerrillas by night instead of armies by day, it is a system which has conscripted vast human and material resources into the building of a tightly knit, highly efficient machine that combines military, diplomatic, intelligence, economic, scientific and political operations".**

> **"Mankind must put an end to war, before war puts an end to mankind".**

> **"If a free society cannot help the many who are poor, it cannot save the few who are rich".**

"As we express our gratitude, we never forget that the highest appreciation is not to utter words, but to live by them".
JFKennedy

The Scotch-Irish Americans have been traditionally lukewarm towards Irish attempts to re-unite the Island of Ireland, choosing instead to support Masonic Brothers in the Orange Order, and preserving the illegal 'act of union' of 1801, which united Irish and English Masons. It is very noticeable when prominent members of Ulster's unionist group visit the USA they are royally wined and dined with brotherly love and assured of friendly media attention, where-as Ulster's nationalists are hounded from pillar to post, forced to suffer hostile and aggressive attention from the hostile media.

Joe Kennedy sr.

President JF Kenndy's father, **Joseph Patrick Kennedy** (September 6, 1888 – November 18, 1969) was an American businessman, investor, and politician known for his high-profile positions in United States government and for the political and other achievements of his children.

Kennedy began his short career in public service in 1934 as the first-ever head of the Securities and Exchange Commission under his long-time friend, President Franklin Delano Roosevelt.

Kennedy's first major involvement in a national political campaign was his support in 1932 for Franklin D. Roosevelt's bid for the Presidency. He donated, loaned, and raised a substantial amount of money for the campaign. Roosevelt rewarded him with an appointment as the inaugural Chairman of the U.S. Securities and Exchange Commission (SEC).

Kennedy's reforming work as SEC Chairman was widely praised on all sides, as investors realized the SEC was protecting their interests. His knowledge of the financial markets enabled him to identify areas requiring the attention of regulators. One of his crucial reforms was the requirement for companies to regularly file financial statements with the SEC which broke what some saw, as an information monopoly maintained by the Morgan banking family. Kennedy left the SEC in 1935 to take over the Maritime Commission, which built on his wartime experience in running a major shipyard. Kennedy eventually resigned from the post, reportedly tired of dealing with unions and ship-owners

Joseph Patrick Kennedy was born into a political family in East Boston, Massachusetts. He made a large fortune as a stock market commodity investor and later rolled over his profits by investing in real estate and a wide range of business industries across the United States. During World War One he was an assistant general manager of the Boston area Bethlehem Steel shipyard; through this position, he became acquainted with Franklin D. Roosevelt, who was the Assistant Secretary of the Navy. In the 1920s, Kennedy made huge profits by reorganizing and refinancing Hollywood studios; several acquisitions were ultimately merged into Radio-Keith-Orpheum (RKO) Studios. Kennedy increased his fortune with distribution rights for Scotch whisky. He owned the largest privately-owned building in the country, Chicago's Merchandise Mart.

Kennedy was a leading member of the Democratic Party and the Irish Catholic community. Kennedy was appointed the first Maritime Commissioner and helped to revive the American shipping industry. Kennedy served as the United States Ambassador to the United Kingdom from 1938 until late 1940, when he annoyed Roosevelt by his pessimism about Britain's survival. During the Battle of Britain in November 1940, Kennedy publicly suggested that "Democracy is finished in England". Following this controversy, Kennedy resigned his position. Did Kennedy foresee democracies evolving into autocracies?

Kennedy had a close friendship with Viscountess Astor and their correspondence is replete with anti-Semitic statements. According to Edward Renehan:

"As fiercely anti-Communist as they were anti-Semitic, Kennedy and Astor looked upon Adolf Hitler as a welcome solution to both of these "world problems", (Nancy's phrase). Kennedy replied that he expected the "Jewish media in the United States to become a problem, as Jewish pundits in New York and Los Angeles were already making noises contrived to "set a match to the fuse of the world"

By August 1940, Kennedy worried that a third term for President Roosevelt would mean war. As Leamer reports, "Joe believed that Roosevelt, Churchill, the Jews, and their allies would manipulate America into approaching Armageddon." Nevertheless, Kennedy supported Roosevelt's third term in return for Roosevelt's promise to support Joseph Kennedy Jr. in a run for Governor of Massachusetts in 1942. However, even during the darkest months of World War II, Kennedy remained "more wary of" prominent American Jews, such as Associate Justice Felix Frankfurter, than he was of Hitler. Felix Frankfurter was born into a Jewish family in Vienna, Austria, on the 15th of November 1882.

Kennedy told the reporter Joe Dinneen:

> "It is true that I have a low opinion of some Jews in public office and in private life. That does not mean that I believe they should be wiped off the face of the Earth. Jews who take an unfair advantage of the fact that theirs is a persecuted race do not help much. Publicizing unjust attacks upon the Jews may help to cure the injustice, but continually publicizing the whole problem only serves to keep it alive in the public mind".

Joe Kennedy's knowledge of the stocks market surely made him wary of doing business with Jews who had friends in high places, particularly on Wall Street.

In view of his attitude towards Jews it is mysterious why he used America's most influential political columnist, Jewish Arthur Krock of *The New York Times*, for decades as a paid speechwriter and political advisor.

Executive Order 11110

There is much speculation as to why President JF Kennedy signed executive order 11110 on June 4, 1963, as the implementation of this Executive Order would effectively neutralise the Federal Reserve Bank and eliminate the national debt.

John F. Kennedy was reared in a family home where the atmosphere was charged with general historical events together with political, business and financial matters. He probably learned much about stock markets, investments, financial trading, loans, interest, pitfalls in banking and political volatility, before he attended his first school. No doubt he also learned about the activities of the greedy and merciless people who stalked Wall Street and the severity of private banks. He learned of insider trading and shady deals and the resulting suffering of marginalised people. Now he was the President and he had the power to make changes to benefit all the people rather than the merciless few. It seems he miscalculated the determination of those who stood to lose much of their money and their consequent loss of power associated with ownership of vast deposits of cash.

As a historical scholar he must have known that:

> Napoleon Bonaparte-(1769-1821) Emperor of France (1804-1815) had a free hand in Europe as long as he borrowed from the Bank of Rothschilds. When he quit borrowing Nathan Rothscilds financed the English who defeated his army at the Battle of Waterloo in 1815. He said: "When a government is dependent upon bankers for money, they, not the leaders of the government control the situation, since the hand that gives is above the hand that takes... Money has no motherland; financiers are without patriotism and without decency; their sole object is gain." Following Napoleon's defeat at waterloo he spent the rest of his life as a prisoner of the British.

President Lincoln needed money to finance the Civil War, and the private syndicated banks offered him loans at 24-36% interest. Lincoln balked at their demands because he didn't want to plunge the nation into such a huge debt. Lincoln approached Congress about passing a law to authorize the printing of U.S. Treasury Notes. Lincoln said "We gave the people of this Republic the greatest blessing they ever had - their own paper money to pay their debts..." Lincoln printed over 400 million "Greenbacks" (debt and interest-free) and paid the soldiers, U.S. government employees, and bought war supplies. The international bankers didn't like it as they wanted Lincoln to borrow the money from them and pay interest on the loans. Lincoln's solution made this seem ridiculous. Shortly after Lincoln's death, the government revoked the Greenback law which ended Lincoln's debt-free, interest-free money. A new national banking act was enacted and all currency became private bank interest-bearing, debt instruments, again.

Before President Garfield was assassinated in 1881 he said that the United States would be seriously disadvantaged if the International Bankers were allowed to freely manage the nation's finances. "Whoever controls the money of a nation controls that nation and is absolute master of all industry and commerce. When you realize that the entire system is very easily controlled, one way or another, by a few powerful men at the top, you will not have to be told how periods of inflation and depression originate."

President William McKinley signed The Gold Standard Act, March 14, 1900 and he was assassinated 14th September 1901 by Leon Czolgoz, who was an admirer of and associated with a Jewish woman named Emma Goldman, a well-known anarchist.

England's Prime Minister Spencer Perceval was preoccupied in 1810-1811 raising funds for England's involvement in the Iberian Peninsular War, economic depression and the bullion controversy in England which threatened to impinge on the Bank of England's profits and his bill was passed to make bank notes legal tender. He was assassinated by John Bellingham in the lobby of the House of Commons on the 15th May 1812.

The assassination of President JF Kennedy has mystified crime scene investigators since that awful day, the 22nd November 1963. There is a theory that he effectively signed his own death warrant when signed Executive Order 11110 which enabled the government to issue its own currency based on the actual amount of silver bullion stocked in the Treasury and four billion dollars in United States $2 and $5 bills were brought into circulation at that time. $10 and $20 bills were being printed at the time of JF Kennedy's assassination but they were never circulated and the $2 and $5 were withdrawn. It is obvious the President was aware that the private Federal Reserve Bank Notes being used as the national currency of the United States was un-Constitutional and he wanted the government to assert its authority and responsibility to regulate its own finances.

Had he lived to see Executive Order 11110 fulfilled, the United States would issue an interest-free and debt-free currency backed by silver reserves in the U.S. Treasury and eventually wipe out the national debt. Following his assassination on the 22nd November 1963, the $2 and $5 United States bills already in circulation were immediately withdrawn giving the Federal Reserve Bank unopposed access to the U.S. monetary market. The silence in the Media regarding the withdrawal, was so deafening, the US people hardly noticed the absence of the $2 and $5 United States notes. The media conveniently ignored the withdrawal of the United States notes while saturating their publications with fake and some accurate reports, theories and speculation regarding the President's assassination.

The president had set a program in train to break the power of the private Federal Reserve banking chain that was financially strangling the American people. He must have known that he was effectively emulating the Nazi financial system that Hitler used in 1935 to create employment, which was such a financial success that it turned insolvent and desolate Germany, into the most financially independent and powerful country in all of Europe, in the space of five years. He must have also known that the Allies had waged a World War to wipe out the Nazis, before they could show the rest of the world how to survive financially, without loans from private banks. Down through history there is abundant evidence of bankers using the power of money to create suitable conditions, both foul and fair, to further increase their monetary reserves.

THE UNITED STATES AND ISRAEL AND IRAQ AFTER 9/11

The U.S.-Israel alliance is rooted in shared Zionist-Masonic values. In the USA in 1899 there were 1,043,800 Jews and in 2014 there were 6,768,855 or 2.1 percent of the total population, 28,000 in Washington DC, or 4.3 percent of Washington DC's state population. The Jewish population in the United States is less than seven million; therefore, the political activity of Jews who view strengthening U.S.-Israel relations to be in the national interest alone, cannot explain the depth of the friendship that exists between them. Fewer than 2 percent of the population could hardly have such a dramatic influence on American national and foreign policies.

"The Israel Lobby in Washington had made considerable progress pushing its agenda during the 1990s even though it was more difficult to make the case that Israel was a strategic asset for the United States once the Cold War was over. Then came the attacks of September 11, 2001, which forced Americans to focus considerable attention on the Arab and Islamic world, and especially the Middle East". 'The Israel Lobby and US foreign policy', by John J. Meaersheimer and Stephen M. Walt.

The Israel Lobby is highly organized and over the years it has established a pressure group within the United States Congress that practically dictates US foreign policy, particularly in relation to the State of Israel and the Middle East in general. They have convinced the American people that the security of Israel and the USA, is under the same perpetual threat from the Arabs and it is seems that they believe, it is necessary to neutralise Palestine, Gaza, Iraq, Syria, Iran and Libya. The Israelis are paranoid about their security probably because they with the support of the, USA, have made little effort to generate friendly relations with their neighbours. In the process of neutralising these states many suspect that they killed Yasser Arafat, Saddam Hussein, Muammar Gaddifa, Ahemd al-Jabari and destabilised the Gaza Strip, Iraq, Libya and Syria and Iran is next on their list. The methods employed by the US and Israel include assassination, extra judicial killing and covert dirty tricks manufactured by the CIA and the Mossad.

The destruction of New York's Twin Towers on the 11th September 2001 killed 2996 and injured more than 6000 people and caused a public outrage that enabled President George Bush to launch a war on Iraq to neutralise Saddam Hussein and Al-Qaeda, both of whom were falsely accused of harbouring weapons for mass destruction. The USA invaded Iraq on the 19th March 2003. Joseph Stiglitz, the Nobel-prize winning economist writing in the Guardian Newspaper says, "The Three Trillion Dollar War reveals the extent to which its effects have been, and will be felt by everyone, from Wall Street to the British high street, from Iraqi civilians to African small traders, for years to come". In addition, "Every household in the United States pays €138 per month towards current operating costs in Iraq" and, "One Trillion Dollars in interest has been paid up to 2017 on the money the US borrowed to finance the war".

Israel together with the USA has been in conflict with Syria since 1948, mainly because they considered Syria was a threat to Israel's security. Syria has not at any time been a military match for Israel and its American supporter. This was very evident during the six-day war in 1967 when the Israeli Military captured Syria and many of the neighbouring Arab countries without significant opposition. The Israelis annexed Syria's beautiful Golan Heights, an area of 1800 square kilometres and expelled 130,000 Syrians. Israel has steadfastly refused to return Golan Heights to Syria in spite of many directives to do so, from the United Nations and the international community. Israeli Prime Minister, Yitzhak Rabin was planning to return the Golan Heights to Syria but he was assassinated before he could do so, in 1995. The Syrian civil war started in 2011 following a youth disturbance which quickly developed into an armed rebellion covertly supported by the CIA, the Mossad, the USA, the UK and crypto Israelis, posing as Syrians. In 2014 Bashar Assad was democratically re-elected in spite of the CIA's efforts to dislodge him by covertly training and arming the rebels at a cost of more than one billion dollars, to date the net result of CIA and

Israeli intervention in Syria has caused the deaths of more than 410,000, more than 1,000,000 wounded, an estimated 5,600,000 refugees and internally displaced 6,600,000 people and has reduced Syria to vast pile of rubble. Israel has refused to admit Syrian refugees.

Jews in Donald Trump's Administration

Jared Corey, Senior Advisor.

Avraham Berkowitz, Special Assist to the President.

David Friedman, Ambassador to Israel.

Jason Greenblatt, Special Representative Israel/Palestine.

Steve Mnuchin, Secretary of the Treasury.

Stephen Miller, Senior Advisor, Policy.

Anne Neuberger, National Security Agency.

Gary Cohn, Director. White House National Economy.

Reed Cordish, Assistant to the president, Technology.

Rod Rosentein, Deputy Attorney General.

Elan Carr, Special envoy to monitor anti-Semitism

Jeffrey A. Rosen, Deputy Secretary Dept; of Transport,

Ezra Cohen, US Dept of Defence, He is opposed to the present Iranian government.

Jared Corey Kushner is a Jewish American investor, real-estate developer and newspaper publisher who is the senior advisor to his father-in-law, US President Donald Trump. Kushner is a son of former real estate developer Charles Kushner the son of Jewish immigrants from the USSR

Jared is married to the president's millionairess daughter Ivanka Trump who has converted to Judaism.

It is remarkable that Trump has not fired any member of his Jewish staff.

The new US Embassy in Jerusalem

Donald Trump's triumphal, opening of the new US Embassy to Jerusalem, in the presence of Jared Corey Kushner and Prime Minister Netanyahu on the 14th May 2018 in front of the Great Seal of the USA, which was prominently displayed in the background, symbolizing the unity of Israel and the United States. This ceremony commemorated the 70th Anniversary of Israel's announcement of nationhood in annexed Palestine in 1948. This day was the bloodiest day of 2018 where more than 40 Palestine protestors were shot dead by the Israelis. Palestinian officials accused the Trump Administration for supporting Israel's claim to Jerusalem.

Donald Trump's United States, on the 25th March 2019, became the only country to recognize Israel's claim of sovereignty over the annexed areas of the **Golan Heights** which Israel conquered in 1967. The European members of the UN Security Council issued a joint statement condemning the US announcement and the UN Secretary-General issued a statement saying that the status of the Golan Heights had not changed. The 28 member states of the European Union declared in turn they do not recognize Israeli sovereignty over the Golan Heights and several experts on international law stated the principle remains that land gained by defensive or offensive wars cannot be annexed under international law. Syria's foreign ministry called the decision a "blatant attack on the sovereignty and territorial integrity" of Syria

This is further evidence of the long standing practice of Zionists working with their Masonic brothers to steal territory surrounding Israel as they have done in America and other places in the last 300 years.

The Israel lobby and the Jewish media, has convinced the USA, the most powerful nation on Earth, that its security depends on Israel, which is one of smallest countries in the world. This has happened because the Zionists and their Masonic brothers have covertly penetrated the upper echelons of the United States Administration and they now secretly dictate foreign policy and legislation.

Agreements negotiated between Israel and the USA has facilitated the housing of weapons of mass destruction on Israeli territory. Known weapons that entered service in 1967 include more than 80 nuclear war heads and mobile intercontinental ballistic missiles entered service in 2008. These missiles in Israel have payloads up to 1300 kg and a range up to 11,500 km and can therefore target sites all over Europe, Asia and Africa. Weapons of mass destruction based in Israel and the USA have the military potential to dominate the entire world.

It is obvious that those who are promoting a New World Order feel it is necessary to build and maintain an indestructible military force to eliminate all possible opposition to their plans.

Because of the USA's endemic relationship with Israel some believe that Israel is the 51st American State and others believe the USA is a Zionist/Masonic colony ruled from its capital city Jerusalem. Either way, the USA is primarily a state within the Zionist - Masonic monetary empire engaged in the art of 'kleptocracy'

Mystical civil wars have erupted in Lebanon and Libya both of which had frequently criticized Israel's treatment of its indigent Arab community and were therefore listed as anti-Semitic and a danger to Israel. Both Lebanon and Libya are now hopelessly divided and economically ruined.

USA AID FOR ISRAEL

The Trump Administration increased The US national debt to $27trillion as of December 2020.

Some economists have estimated: That, since 1949 the United States has aided Israel with a total of $83.205 billion, which attracted $49,937 billion interest that U.S. tax payers naively paid on behalf of Israel, bringing the total aid given to Israel since 1949 to $1.33132 billion. This means that U.S. has given more federal aid to Israeli citizens annually than it has given to the average American citizen.

Because The United States is effectively a Masonic cum Zionist colony, it is no mystery why they have continued to pour money without conditions, into the rogue state of Israel that ignores international law, steals neighbouring land, practices extrajudicial assassination, a possessor of weapons of mass destruction and is engaged in ethnic cleansing of non-Jewish residents in Israel.

Mount Rushmore's Masonic Monument was the obvious place for Donald Trump to canvass Freemasons on July the 4th 2020. **"Today, we pay tribute to the exceptional lives and extraordinary legacies of George Washington, Thomas Jefferson, Abraham Lincoln, and Teddy Roosevelt, I am here as your President to** proclaim before the country and before the world: This monument will never be desecrated, these heroes will never be defaced, their legacy will never, ever be destroyed, their achievements will never be forgotten, and Mount Rushmore will stand forever as an eternal tribute to our forefathers and to our freedom".

THE HOLOCAUST INDUSTRY

In a controversial new study, Norman G. Finkelstein moves from an interrogation of the place, the Holocaust has come to occupy in American culture, to a disturbing examination of recent Holocaust compensation agreements.

It was not until the Arab-Israeli War of 1967, when Israel's evident strength brought it into line with US foreign policy. Memory of the Holocaust began to acquire the exceptional prominence it enjoys today. Leaders of American's Jewish community were delighted that Israel was now deemed a major strategic asset and they exploited the Holocaust to enhance this new-found status. Their subsequent interpretations of the tragedy are often at variance with actual historical events and are employed to deflect any criticism of Israel and its supporters.

Recalling Holocaust hoaxers such as Jerzy Kosinski and Binjamin Wilkomirski, as well as the demagogic constructions of writers like Daniel Goldhagen, Finkelstein contends that the main danger posed to the memory of Nazism's victims, comes not from the distortions of Holocaust deniers but from self-proclaimed guardians of Holocaust memory. Drawing on a wealth of untapped sources, he exposes the double shakedown of European countries, as well as legitimate Jewish claimants, and concludes that the Holocaust industry has become an outright extortion racket.

"I filed the first suit against the Swiss banks for Holocaust compensation. The truth about the compensation monies must be told. Holocaust survivors, many living in poverty, have been cheated by major Jewish organizations. Documentation relating to this scandal is being ignored. Norman Finkelstein finally breaks the silence. I urge everyone to read this book to learn the real story of our suffering." Gizella Weissaus.

'The Holocaust Industry' by Norman Finkelstein.

The Terrible Power of the Purse.

Reflecting on Jewish-Zionists and Masonic involvement in the wars listed herein, it becomes obvious that the 'power of money' promoted each and every conflict. Recount the 'the terrible power of the purse' employed to successfully achieve their planned objectives to regain investments, buying low and selling high in the wake of wars and other disasters, increasing their mountain of cash. The continuous use of the power of money within Judaism, has discredited and isolated Jews from the mainstream of humanity, since Judas betrayed Jesus for thirty pieces of Silver.

The wastage of human resources and the miss-use of Money has brought about a world of human misery, hunger, degradation, human baseness, avarice, violence. Our world has been saturated with guns and military hardware, purported for defence purposes but in reality to enable nations to make war on their neighbours. To be totally secure it is necessary to be better armed than your neighbour, this in turn creates 'an arms race' i.e. a demand for more and better arms, creates investment opportunities for financiers and round and round to story goes creating mountains of cash for 'money gluttons'. Oxfam has found that: **The combined wealth of the 80 richest billionaires, (eight of which are Americans) is the same amount as that of the bottom 50% of the Earth's population.**

The Zionist/Masonic media have continually published details of the numbers of Jews who were killed in WW1 and WW2, while ignoring the number Freemasons who were also killed in the same wars. It may be considered to be unproductive to discuss this in public, because many Jews were executed, not solely because they were Jews but because they members of the Freemasonry organisation which was outlawed by the Nazis.

The Zionist/Masonic media refrain from publishing real details about the estimated 70 million Christian deaths, both military and civilian, from all the European countries and the USA, in WW1 and WW2. Perhaps it is advantageous if divided Christians eliminate each other.

THE BEEHIVE IS A FREEMASONRY SYMBOL

SOCIAL STRUCTURE OF THE HONEY BEE

Freemasons are fascinated by the social structure of honey bees. An average of 30,000 bees inhabits a typical hive and each bee performs a very specific function within the group. Honey bee colonies are very efficient organizations, where members are programmed for breeding, collecting nectar, maintaining the hive or processing the collected nectar in the hive. All of the bees have communication skills that coordinate the productivity of the entire hive.

Each hive has a Queen

The queen is a matriarch and everything revolves around her, however her main purpose is to populate the colony. She can lay as many 15,000 eggs per day and in addition she produces a pheromone which is necessary to unite the colony. The worker bees scrupulously attend to her every need and feed her with royal jelly. They also build the hexagonal honeycomb cells for her new born eggs which they take from the queen and place them in the cells to incubate. They also take care of the larvae.

All activities and work done inside the hive and the labour of those on the outside, who forage far and wide collecting precious honey and pollen, is carried out with absolute obedience, in a benign and peaceful atmosphere. It is the desired format for human labour relationships in industrial establishments to produce the best profits. The honey bee colony is a source of endless fascination and a model of teamwork.

According to the philosophy of Freemasonry, the word "industry" denotes manufacturing and factories classified as heavy industry and light industry ages before the availability of heavy machinery that vast building enterprises were accomplished. The mystery of such accomplishments intrigued Masonic employers and wondered how the Egyptian builders motivate large numbers of workers to build the pyramids and the ancient

Egyptian canals They learned that Egyptians used the Beehive as symbol of team work and considered it to be the perfect emblem of the power of industry, because what no one bee or a number of individual bees could accomplish, becomes easy when the entire hive works together on any single job. (such as Henry Ford's masonic assembly line).

The ritual of a Freemasonry Lodge is organised around forms of work, where members occupy places and locations which signify the importance of the power of industry, symbolised by the beehive and its hierarchy, from which the Masonic work philosophy developed a fraternal fellowship regarding the economics of work and the rewards embedded therein.

They are keenly aware of the relationship between work and money. They know that all wealth is generated from all forms of labour, from menial tasks to top class engineers and scientists. The Masonic Zionist Alliance's control of the global financial system has also enabled them to control the labour markets. They have learned the lucrative benefits of employing women and they have developed a range of incentives to encourage them to remain childless enabling them to remain at the grindstone without maternal absences. In many industries employers provide abortion services in order to retain women in the workforce. They have also separated mothers from their children, financially binding them to the grindstone in order to generate more wealth. They brought about the situation where it takes the joint income of fathers and mothers, to maintain crippling mortgages. Traditionally, the father alone earned enough money to keep a roof over their heads.

Freemasonry stresses the importance of fraternal cooperation to achieve the maximum rewards from all forms of work, particularly the construction of large State financed structures, inspired and facilitated by Masonic members within governments. The financial benefits are enormous when Masonic brothers are involved at every level, from conception to completion, where each and every brother involved in the project receives a generous share of allocated finances.

It is remarkable that Masonic financial and other companies use the beehive or other Masonic symbols as logos, indicating to their Masonic brothers that they will receive extra Masonic benefits in their dealings with such companies.

Freemasons secretly recognise that a man's labour is the alchemy that not only mines gold but produces wealth and services of all kinds.

Freemasons must swear an oath to a nondescript creator that is not the triune God, which excludes Jesus Christ.

It is well known that most of the Christians in the USA including Roman Catholics, Evangelical, Lutherans and Orthodox churches forbid membership in Freemasonry because it is incompatible with Jesus Christ.

A Masonic Lodge is held to be a deistic religious organization that requires members to believe that entrance into the 'hereafter' is gained by following the precepts and morality of Freemasonry, that a God of their choice will let them into heaven merely because they have been faithful Masons. Every Masonic ritual involves prayer to a member's personal God and every meeting involves ritual. They refer to their lodges as temples. Every Masonic lodge has an altar in the centre of the room, with a Bible or another holy book placed upon it, at which many prayers to the Great Architect are prayed.

Mackey has this to say about the Masonic altar. ***"From all this we can see that the altar in Freemasonry is not merely a convenient article of furniture, intended like a table, to hold a Bible. It is a sacred utensil of religion, intended, like the altars of the ancient temples, for religious uses, and thus identifying Freemasonry, by its necessary existence in our lodges, as a religious institution. Its presence should also lead the contemplative Freemason, to view the ceremonies in which it is employed with solemn reverence, as being part of a really religious worship"*** *(Mackey: 56).*

On the contrary, we contend, without any sort of hesitation, that Freemasonry is, in every sense of the word except one, and that it's least philosophical, an eminently religious institution—that it is indebted solely to the religious element it contains for its origin as well as its continued existence... The tendency of all Freemasonry is toward religion. If it makes any progress, its progress is toward that holy end. Look at its ancient landmarks, its sublime ceremonies, its profound symbols and allegories—all inculcating religious doctrine, commanding religious observance, and teaching religious truth, and who can deny that it is eminently a religious Institution. . . . We open and close our Lodges with prayer; we invoke the presence of the Most High upon all our labours; we demand of our neophytes a profession of trusting belief in the existence and the superintending care of God; and we teach them to bow with humility and reverence at His awful name., while His holy Law is widely opened upon our altars" (Mackey: 847).

According to Mackey's definition, Freemasons consider their rituals to be religious in every sense of the word but the absence of Jesus Christ in their doctrines tends to place their religious values in the Old Testament while ignoring the tenets of Jesus Christ in the New Testament. Their adherence to the values of the Old Testament cunningly facilitates Zionist-Freemasons who continue to practice all the pre-Christian vices which Jesus rejected.

Ten Popes have condemned the Society of Freemasons. Pope Leo XIII warned his bishops:

> *"Tear away the mask of Freemasonry and make plain to all what it is. It aims at the utter overthrow of the whole religious order of the world which Christian teaching has produced, and the substitution of a new state of things, based on the principles of pure naturalism. Including almost every nation in its grasp it unites itself with other sects of which it is the real inspiration and hidden motive power. It first attracts and then retains its associates by the bait of worldly advantage which it secures for them. It bends governments to its will, sometime by promises, other times by threats. It has found its way into every class of society and forms an invisible and irresponsible power, an independent government as it were within the body corporate of the lawful state. It denies that our first parents sinned, and consequently that man's free will is in any way weakened or inclined to evil. Wherefore we see that men are publicly tempted by the many allurements of pleasure, that there are journals or pamphlets without moderation or shame, that stage plays are remarkable in licence, that designs for works of art are shamelessly sought in the laws of so-called realism...and that all the blandishments of pleasure are diligently sought out by which virtue may be lulled to sleep. There have been*

> *in these secret societies some who have proposed*
> *artfully and of set purpose, that the multitude*
> *should be satiated with a boundless licence of*
> *vice, as when this had been done it could come*
> *more easily under their power and authority".*

Orthodox Jews, have traditionally opposed the activities of the Zionists; however, some of them have been converted and now accept Zionist philosophy. Rabbinical authorities have led the Jewish people of the world for 2000 years. When Zionism first appeared it was seen as a distinct rejection of their authority and Orthodox law. The Zionist ambition to create a settlement for Judaism in Palestine would abandon the Yeshiva seminaries and the synagogue. The radical Zionist program planned to force the hand of Providence and to contradict the teachings of Orthodox Judaism regarding the coming of the Messiah and the Restoration. In Western Europe the Ashkenazy Jews held these views but the Sephardic Jews offered no opposition to the proposed Palestine Settlement or to the Zionists.

> *"The Judaeo-Christian tradition' turns*
> *out to be no empty phrase. It refers, at least*
> *in part, to a morality that can survive apart*
> *from religious faith. Like Christianity, 'true*
> *Torah Judaism' sees pride not as a virtue but*
> *as a cardinal sin. More important, the orthodox*
> *creed insists that Jews have not inherited some*
> *moral carte blanche from their sufferings. They*
> *should not advertise their victimhood or promote*

themselves. Instead of trumpeting 'their' achievements—as if the accomplishments of brilliant Jews were some badge of racial superiority—they should take responsibility for their misdeeds. They should seek, not power, but to live peaceably with others, not in 'their own state' (the orthodox view states and peoples with just suspicion) but in whatever state they find themselves to be. In other words much of what is labelled 'anti-Semitic' by Zionists today—the denial of the specialness of the Jewish people or of any sense of entitlement proceeding from their sufferings—becomes, in the light of orthodox critiques of Zionism, something much closer to ordinary morality". [12]

---

[12] Jewish opposition to Zionism by Michael Neumann.

THE RISE OF THE
JEWISH-MASONIC ALLIANCE

In spite of the widespread opposition and downright condemnation of the Zionist-Masonic alliance, the movement has continued to expand and prosper in all spheres of national and international activities, political, legal, cultural, economic, religious, construction, education, the media and finance in particular. Any event, wars in particular, that offer, opportunities to make a monetary gain is graciously accepted. Members of the alliance are involved through their lodges in every possible sector of everyday living like parasites gnawing on their victims. They make money by tearing apart and in building up. They have been involved in all the revolutions and in all the wars of the last two hundred and fifty years and they have made money from each and every conflict. The Zionist-Masonic alliance has psychically ingratiated itself to the general public to such an extent, that they are able to penetrate and control every public and private department in most of the western countries They have historically succeeded in having their members elected to all the western governments, a brief examination of the profiles of members of government, presidents of universities, private corporations, will confirm this assertion. They also work to be elected to each and every local organization such as town councils, golf clubs, school boards, development committees, etc.; and often they are able to swing a vote to suit themselves at meetings and any useful information gathered is reported to brother members at lodge meetings. This is how they keep themselves fully informed about everything that may be going down in their own localities, giving them the edge to act when it may benefit their own interests. Their involvement in education and with local communities further enables them to spot young people, men in particular, who have special talents and potential that would enhance the Masons. . These young men are usually recruited and offered enticements join the Masons, with promises to promote and provide them with opportunities to excel and when they become household icons, the Masons often reveal them as members, conveying to the public a picture of Masonic beauty, genius and as major contributors to the well-being of the community and the nation. These members however, will always be beholden to the Masons, never really sure if they could have made it on their own and of course there is always a pay-back by way of heavy contributions.

The majority of Freemasons on the lower levels of the society are oblivious to what that organization is really doing. They are manipulated foot soldiers and a largely drip-fed from the secret few who control this vast secret society. When the Zionist-Masonic society is accused of conspiring to control the people of the world, it is important to remember that the lower Masonic and Jewish members are merely the programmed workers bees who bring in the honey but the society's power is in the hands of the leaders (the few).

The traditional pursuit of the Zionist – Masonic Alliance has mainly been in the realm of finance. They have developed systems to cream off percentages of all the money that is processed in their banks and having assured most sovereign governments that they will keep and provide records of all banking transactions if ordered to do so by the courts and thereby receive a measure of financial independence.

Their connection with national governments effectively places them above the law. Their formula mirrors the conman's philosophy, "**I have no desire to rob anyone of a million dollars but I have no problem taking one dollar from each of a million people**". The banks are using this formula every second, night and day by taking a small cut from millions of card and other small transactions. They are immoral, arrogant and greedy. They pay themselves enormous salaries and bonuses without regard to wage earners who will be forever suffering austerity unless they find a way to reap a fair share for their labour. The wealthiest individuals and families in the world are all linked, in one way or another to the Freemasons or the Zionists or to both of them. Their combined activities in the financial world has brought them mountains of cash, which they use to control goods, services, industrial output, etc.; etc.; etc:

Their domination of governments is so complete that they virtually decide in minute detail all the activities of populations, from 'their rising up to their going down'. Their control of the media alters the people's thought processes, morality, relationships, and sexuality, etc; etc:

Few consider Judaism in missionary terms but that is principally what they are about. Their mission has a structure which is not only a self-financing operation but it is also a money-making business, selling their philosophy to their converts and addicts. Jews do not accept that Jesus Christ is their promised Messiah and they do not consider themselves bound by any of the Christian Precepts. St Paul wrote, 1 Corinthians 1:22-25 "We are preaching a crucified Christ; to the Jews, an obstacle that they cannot get over..." They continue to practice and promote the laws and doctrines of the Old Testament, e.g. Jesus rejected the law of; 'A tooth for a tooth an eye for an eye, hand for hand, foot for foot, life for life', (In recent Israeli Palestinian skirmishes in Gaza, for every Israeli death, there was an average of 23 Palestinian deaths). Their missionary objective is not to religiously convert the whole world to Judaism but to control and subdue the global population by subjecting them to pecuniary Jewish laws and monetary philosophy. They have largely achieved their object through a continuous bombardment, of the desirability of base human appetites, in Hollywood films, TV and the printed Media. Israel and the USA have no moral objection to 'extra judicial killing' and outright assassination. The Jewish practice of usury has virtually enslaved the whole world, e.g. to give someone a mortgage is like shackling a slave with a ball and chain, the borrower and his wife must now get up and go to work every day, to earn money to pay the mortgage instalments and his employer must also pay a share of the profits generated by his employees to his Jewish-Masonic financier. The modern financial system is such that, most people can never save enough money to buy a house, which dictates that it is necessary to enter into a mortgage to secure a home. This person is the modern slave earning money for the richest people in the world. The Zionists and the Masons have insidiously worked their way into the top echelons of every branch of western society and industry. Their controlling presence in the USA administration is common knowledge, e.g. they were able to arrange for the Prime Minister of Israel to address Congress on the 3rd March 2015 without President Obama's knowledge or consent. Jews in the American administration are more inclined to accept information from Israel's secret service the Mossad, than from the CIA, particularly in matters relating to the Middle-East.

Everyone knows that the Jews control Hollywood but few are aware, that it really is a Zionist-Masonic association that is actually pulling the strings. Together they have been pumping Zionist-Masonic philosophy and values, around the world for more than one hundred years, as the supposed imaginative inventions of script writers, which are generally anti-Christian. Careful analysis of their Hollywood films will reveal their promotion, of extra-judicial killing, assassination, mistreatment of women, advocacy of illicit sex, glorification of war and violence, approval of sharp practices in business and personal relationships, justifying a 'right' to tell lies, oblique downgrading of Catholicism, insertion of Masonic and Jewish philosophy and symbols into film productions, undoubtedly to convey secret messages to their 'brethren' that might be in the audience, particularly to those who had bought shares in the production on screen, disrespect and deliberate misinterpretation of native people's culture, religion and customs, excesses in the use of food and drinking of alcohol, promotion of tobacco and drugs, and other products of 'brother' investors by giving them free innocuous exposure on screen, such as actors smoking cigarettes, the **secret practice of promoting** Jewish and Masonic actors while abusing gentile men and women actors, support for Jews and Masons in politics, medicine, industry, education, military and finance. The zeal of Zionists and Masons to promote their moral values, can only be described as a most successful mission to convert the whole world into a single, unified race of unloving slavish people, who live lives of personal gratification and unlimited selfishness, the abandonment of traditional family values, where domestic abuse, rape, incest, robbery, violence, depression, hopelessness, loneliness, suicide, hunger, imprisonment, addiction and drug related disease is very much in evidence. All this emanating from the Zionist Masonic media's efforts, to neutralise Jesus Christ and Christian family values, while promoting base sexual temptations, base appetites for food and base inclinations of human beings, as forecasted in the 'Alta Vendita'. They do indeed, "broadcast vice among the multitude to breathe it in through their five senses and become saturated with it, making human hearts corrupt and vicious, drawing them away from their Christian faith by filling their minds and occupying their time with other matters, separating them from the Church". Indeed the corruption in the media is not only affecting Christians but every other religious group and even those who have no religion. If large numbers of people leave the Churches, Christianity will decay and cease to be a force for love, goodness, harmony, peace and justice, giving the Zionists and the Masons freedom to continue their mission to promote a world of greed, conflict and corruption unopposed. A combined Christian force of all those who follow Jesus Christ, is needed to combat the influence of those who are actively working to neutralize Him. To counteract the oppression caused by money gurus, Christians must develop new systems to escape the guru's oppression of humanity and learn that the money that gurus use is generated by the oppressed. Gurus then use this money to cause further oppression to increase their monetary profits. This is a study, of the power of money being used to make war, to oppress nations, to pollute environments, to manufacture weapons of mass destruction and deliberately endanger planet earth, in order to acquire more and more money.

JESUS CHRIST IS CEO OF GOD'S ECONOMY

Jesus Christ was the first globalist and His New Covenant of salvation promised by God to humans individually, is based on divine grace rather than Mosaic Law. The New Covenant may be described as a New World Order established from the tenets of Jesus Christ's manifesto contained in the Gospels and the letters of Saint Paul. His manifesto broadly guarantees salvation to all those who practice and live according to His terms and conditions contained therein. Awareness of God in prayer requires a benign attitude, a willingness to forgive the repentant, to share and pool resources, to recognise and help our needy sisters and brothers, a readiness to turn the other cheek, to willingly go an extra mile, practice self-discipline, personal sacrifice and strong faith, show kindness and unconditional love and seek forgiveness for personal wrong doing and remember always His promise: **"Where two or more are gathered together in my mane I will be there in the midst of them"**.

In the Caesar teaching Jesus Christ promoted a monetary program for His followers to fulfil God's need of money. Those who preach the Gospel should clearly convey the economic importance, of the difference between giving money to Caesar and giving the money to God. Giving money to God enables Him through all those who believe in Him to fulfil the corporal works of mercy and to spread the 'good news'. Giving money to Caesar supports uncorrupted democracy and the common good.

A great omission of the Catholic Hierarchy is their mysterious failure to develop a theology on the sanctity money which is the fruit of human work, the sacred means of fulfilling and achieving the universal love of God. The negligence of Christian hierarchies to sanctify human work and its monetary fruit, has allowed the enemies of Jesus Christ to prosper and debase the world from a place of beauty to an ugly place of horrendous, harrowing and atrocious living conditions, for a vast number of undernourished and oppressed people

Christians appear to have no concept of the spirituality of money, in spite of the fact, that Jesus Christ spoke so much about it, more often than He spoke about prayer and faith combined. Eleven of His parables were lessons about money and associated spiritual truths.

Timid and financially naïve people throughout the world have failed, to recognise the insidious evil programmes and the wars financed by those who disregard Jesus Christ's teaching, regarding the people's money. Being unaware of the evil intentions of those who largely rule the financial world, Christians and other faiths have been duped by the financial institutions that mislead depositors, causing them to believe that their money would be used for the common good and world peace.

It is necessary to compound a new Christian theology to clarify Jesus Christ's many references to work and money, in order to spiritually encourage Christians and all who have compassion for the needy, to sacrifice at least 10% of their discretionary income and/or free time, to support God's work among those who need food, water, shelter and so much more.

Ordinary people working in all spheres are together the source of all the wealth in the world and they largely have similar spiritual philosophies regarding the welfare of people everywhere, however, their inability to work in unison, has caused widespread degradation of humanity in general and the human family in particular. If by some miracle they could all work together, according to Jesus Christ's instructions, this world would be a utopia. Were, it possible, that every community in the world could accept, that Jesus loves all of them and He has no plan to destroy their laws or their leaders, for He did not come to destroy their laws or their prophets, He came to fulfil". If only all communities could take some time to examine Jesus' manifesto and compare it to their own laws and rituals, and assess, if their relationships and living conditions could be universally improved.

> *It appears the Catholic Church has failed to recognise that there are evil people inside and outside the Church causing division and confusion while mingling freely within the human race at all levels:*

*i.e. religions, governments, civil services, the Media, finance, banking, entertainment, education, military and industry, in spite of the clear teaching of Jesus Christ when He warned: "Look for the wolves in sheep's clothing". "A bad tree cannot bear good fruit". "By their fruits you will know them". We know that he was accosted on many occasions by evil people with evil intentions and He gave His followers, the **Lord's Prayer (The Our Father),** which concludes....**deliver us from evil**".*

Jesus gave His Church a clear mandate to mount intensive campaigns against evil, to make the whole world aware of evilness and to rescue those who have been touched by it and to convince those in power who have been promoting evilness to repent and broadcast goodness instead. The Church must develop a new awareness of the' wolves in sheep's clothing' within its own ranks and elsewhere and deprive them of the power to contaminate others...Taylor Marshall's 'INFILTRATION'.

"Beloved, let us love one another, for love is of God; and everyone who is born of God and knows God. He who does not love, does not know God, for God is love". John 1-4:7

[36] "Teacher, which is the greatest commandment in the Law?"

[37.] Jesus replied: "Love the Lord your God with all your heart and with all your soul and with all your mind.

[38] This is the first and greatest commandment.

[39] And the second is like it: 'Love your neighbour as yourself.

[40] All the Law and the Prophets hang on these two commandments. Matt 22-36:40.

To love yourself, you must educate yourself, preserve your mental health, nourish your body and do no harm to yourself. To love your neighbours do likewise for them.

Have we failed to understand the ultimate power of the love that Jesus Christ taught us? To be a true follower of Jesus, it is necessary to fully understand and come to terms with the love God bestows and the love He demands of those who believe in Him. This raises the question, what exactly is the love that Jesus spoke of so often? **Prayer begets love, love begets work and work begets money to finance more work**. Love mentally recognises and assesses a need and work fulfils that need. Love is His gift of a 'two-way' blessing. When one becomes aware of the constancy of His love and recognise His loving presence in all creation, one will surely love Him in return.

EUCHARIST AND TRANSSUBSTANTIATION

The doctrine of transubstantiation, elaborated by Scholastic theologians from the 13th to the 15th century, was incorporated into the documents of the Council of Trent (1545–63). The faith in the real presence as brought about by a mysterious change, antedates the Scholastic formulation of the doctrine, as is shown by the use of equivalent terms in the patristic writers. In the mid-20th century some Roman Catholic theologians restated the doctrine of Christ's eucharistic presence. Shifting the emphasis from a change of substance to a change of meaning, they coined the terms, transsignification and transfinalization to be used in preference to transubstantiation. But, in his encyclical Mysterium fidei in 1965, Pope Paul VI called for a retention of the dogma of real presence together with the terminology of transubstantiation in which it had been expressed Encyclopaedia Britannica

Some believe that because of His omnipresence, Christ is already present in bread and wine before the consecration as He is in all creation. "By nature God is present in all things by essence, knowledge and power. This is the presence of a cause in the things that share in God's goodness. By his essence, he is substantially in all things, including the created spiritual essences as the immediate origin of their existence, by his knowledge, he exercises his wisdom directly in all creation down to the least details. By his power, he operates with divine activity as the First Cause of everything that creatures do". The Catholic dictionary.

Jesus called His disciples together in the 'Upper Room' on Mount Zion near Jerusalem to partake in His 'Last Supper'. Towards the end of the supper, He took bread, blessed and broke it, and giving it to them said: "Take and eat; this is My body"; then He took a cup of wine, blessed it, and giving it to them, said: "All of you drink of this; for this is My blood of the new covenant which is being shed for many unto the forgiveness of sins". Finally, He commissioned His disciples, "Do this in remembrance of me".

John 6:53-56. "Then Jesus said to them, "Most assuredly, I say to you, unless you eat the flesh of the Son of Man and drink His blood, you have no life in you. [54] Whoever eats My flesh and drinks My blood has eternal life, and I will raise him up at the last day. [55] For My flesh is food indeed and My blood is drink indeed. [56] He who eats My flesh and drinks My blood abides in Me, and I in him".

An informal Eucharistic Celebration

When Jesus said; "My body is real food and my blood is real drink", was He using a metaphor to tell His followers that he is totally and forever present in all food and in all drink and by extension He is also present in all creation. His presence is thereby visible in mankind and the environment, which is His sacred, holy and spiritual home on earth, where He sustains humanity and all living things. To believe that everything in the environment is His body and blood, is to accept that He was put there by God for the spiritual and temporal benefit of the human race according to their needs. The fact that most people eat and drink several times each day, provides them with an opportunity to consciously recall, that they are Eucharistically eating His body and drinking His blood. There is great joy in knowing that everything one eats, drinks, touches, hears, sees, smells, tastes and uses from the environment is His flesh and blood, which enables His followers to abide in Him and He in them. When Christians consciously gather together in His name to share a meal they should remember His promise, to be in midst of them and they should always provide a chair at the table for Jesus to sit upon. Being conscious of Jesus' omnipresence each and every activity will be done in His name and His followers are likely to adhere to His teaching, to repent and seek His forgiveness for personal wrong doing. They will love God, love one's own body and love one's neighbour accordingly. Jesus Christ made it abundantly clear, that fulfilling the spiritual and temporal needs of others and every living thing, is the way to salvation and eternal life.

"I have come that they may have life, and have it to the full." John 10:10

'Man shall not live by bread alone, but by every word that proceeds from the mouth of God." Matt, 4:4.

Consciousness of Jesus Christ's omnipresence supplies spiritual, psychical, and physical energy every human needs to create a world free from hunger and violence, a world filled with prayer, love and joyful work.

In believing that God is present in all food and drink, it is also necessary to believe that He is present, in all the living things that must die, in order to sustain the lives of other living things, including human beings. Believing God is truly present in all living things, confirms the spirituality of all life on earth. The people, who are conscious of the spiritual origin of every mouthful of food and every drop they drink, will also be conscious of God's need for the cooperative work of His followers to cultivate and produce food and drink for everyone.

Was He also telling His followers that all dining rituals, whether private, family or public, should be reflections of His Last Supper and celebrated in exactly the same manner, so that His followers would be always conscious of His omnipresence in the food and drink on the table before them and they should consciously eat and drink, while meditating on the Divine source of the food and drink which sustains all living things and thanking God for His bounty and the work of all the human hands that brought it to the table?

A formal Eucharistic Celebration

The Sunday Mass should be seen as a formal Eucharist celebration for the entire community to ritually consume small portions food and drink of individual choice which members bring with them to represent His body and blood and omnipresence in daily food and drink, while offering to sacrifice themselves as servants of God and humanity, in remembrance of Jesus Christ's Last Supper and His sacrifice on the cross.

The Second Vatican Council's Constitution on the Sacred Liturgy No. 48: says, the faithful should be "conscious" participants "by offering the Immaculate Victim, not only through the hands of the priest, but also with him, they should learn also to offer themselves.".

When Jesus instituted the Holy Eucharist during His Last Supper, He radically chose two labour intensively manufactured food items, bread and wine, and declared them to be His body and blood. His implicit declaration thereby endorsed human work, as the divine activity which forms the core of humanity's connection to God.

While contemplating the necessary work of human hands and minds that is required to produce a loaf of bread and a bottle of wine, it becomes clear, that it all begins by tilling the soil, sowing the seeds, planting the vines, protecting and weeding the plants, harvesting the grain and the grapes, threshing the corn, pressing the grapes, milling the grain, fermenting the wine, mixing the dough, providing an oven together with fuel to bake the bread, providing vats to process the grapes, straining the wine, providing receptacles to store the wine. It is fitting that the **work** of human hands is recognized in the liturgy of the Eucharist:-

> *Blessed are you, Lord God of all creation, for through your goodness we have received the bread we offer you: fruit of the earth and work of human hands, it will become for us the bread of life.*

> *Blessed are you, Lord God of all creation, for through your goodness we have received the wine we offer you: fruit of the vine and work of human hands, it will become our spiritual drink.*

Jesus could have chosen a whole fruit to eat and water to drink and thereby exclude the work of human hands but He chose bread and wine, and thereby, integrally connected human **work** to the Eucharist. The Eucharist is principally a celebration of the fact that Jesus sacrificed himself to affirm His New Covenant and commanded His followers to serve God by sacrificing themselves through their work for their own benefit, the benefit of others and the glory of God. The fundamental sacrifice of human beings is their work, in all its forms.

In Jesus Christ, prayer is sacred, love is sacred, human work is sacred, it follows that money is also sacred, because it is the product of work.

There is a tragic void, between the sacrifice on the altar and sacrifice within the pews, something like a 'we and they' distinction. It is tragic because the solution is so simple.

The celebrating priest should remind the congregation at the beginning of Mass that Jesus promised to be present in midst of those who are gathered together in His name. This surely and expressly applies to those attending Mass to celebrate the Eucharistic Sacrifice, during which they should be encouraged to offer themselves and their work as sacrifices and the grace God would descend in a warm spiritual aura on all of them.

Were it permissible for the priest to ritually recognise the sacrifices of the laity, their physical efforts to attend Mass, their contributions of voluntary work and money earned from work, done in the name of God to support their families, for the good of His Church and for the needy, it would substantiate the laity's integration in the Holy Eucharist and would also verify the spirituality of the people's enterprise beyond the confines of the Chapel,. This would create a conscious recognition of the spirituality embedded in work, the workplace and the environment, in keeping with the teaching of Jesus Christ and Pope Francis' Laudato Si, and Fratelli Tutti and an awareness of the omnipresence of Jesus and the spirituality of all things. This would surely appeal to everyone, young people in particular, as it would give them a spiritual reason to use their talents to improve living conditions at home and abroad. Those who consciously work for Jesus experience happy emotions of wellbeing following the completion of each and every task done in His name.

The missal ritual prayer: *'Pray, brothers and sisters, that my sacrifice and yours may be acceptable to God, the almighty Father'* would take on real meaning if the people's contributions of work and money were ritually recognized as sacrifices of women, men and especially children in particular.

It is through their **work** the laity can be finally united with God. It is by sacrificing themselves through their work, they show their love for God, humanity and all creation. Nothing can be achieved without **work**, it is the most precious thing that people possess and consequently it is the greatest Sacrifice they can offer to God, and it should be recognised as such in Eucharistic rituals. Jesus encouraged His followers to serve God through personal sacrifice. Opportunities for personal sacrifice are all embracing:

turn the other cheek, sacrificing your right-of-way on the road, disregarding insults, practicing humility and moderation, doing 'works of mercy, volunteering labour, donating money, etc.: People work to earn money and unselfishly share their earnings with family, government, the poor and the Church. At present it is all done in a sort of a pagan vacuum, as there are no established Catholic rituals celebrating the work of the Laity. It is so sad that no special recognition given to the spirituality of the Laity's sacrifices in the Liturgy of the Eucharist and it is noticeable where members of the congregation, present gifts of bread, wine together with the collection before the Offertory, the priest does not give the collection the same reverence as he does to the bread and wine, at best it is usually passed to a server without comment and placed at the foot of the altar, like someone receiving an unwanted or a soiled gift. The Sunday Mass collection and other donations are considerable sacrifices of the Laity and are tangible expressions of their love, the work of their hands and minds, which should be placed on the altar and incorporated into the liturgy of the Eucharist, perhaps as follows:-

> *"Blessed are you, Lord, God of all creation we have sacrifices of work and money to offer you, which your people have given at your command, the work of their hands and minds to support their families, needy brothers and sister, for the wellbeing of our Holy Catholic Church and for justice in civil authorities".*

This would create an integral connection between the congregation and the sacred celebration and confirm work is a holy and spiritual activity that is necessary to achieve Jesus' command to spread the 'Good News' to all of mankind, for the peace and wellbeing of all creation. It would be a spiritual recognition of the supreme sacrificial work of parents who diligently beget and rear their children and all the other daily sacrifices the laity make while doing God's work. It would promote a spiritual work ethic. The people's money is sacred, because it is the spiritual element of their work and it should be included ritually in the celebration of the mass, tangibly connecting their sacrifice to the sacrifice of Jesus. This would give the Mass, an added spiritual purpose and direction. Every person would thereby be a constituent part of the Mass through their sacrificial work. The laity would recover the long lost spiritual connection of, prayer, love, work, and money, which is the Holy Grail of Christianity. Money in the hands God's people can manufacture and cure all things. In evil hands it can destroy things.

Global-warming is due to Evil people using money for evil purposes. "By their fruits you will know them" Matt 7:16.20. If Christians wish to save our planet they must learn to keep their money out of evil hands by refusing to work on evil projects and learn to recognise the God given supreme power that is embedded in their money. A power to establish Heaven on Earth.

Labour is Raw Material!

St John Paul II said; "money is heaped up labour". There has been a value on a person's labour since the beginning of time. Focus on any manmade object in your line of sight and you may conclude, it was manufactured from God given raw material, which may be animal, mineral or vegetable, or combination thereof. Raw material has been present on earth since God created the world and it belongs to everyone but it was of little value until man began working, to convert this material into useful things, which then acquired a monetary value in proportion to the amount of labour employed in the manufacturing process. Initially labour was bartered as a day's work being exchanged for a day's work. At some point in time, money became the universal standard of labour, inaugurating the unhappy practice of storing labour in the form of money. Labour thus became a commercial unit, which could be bought and sold in the form of money, and was eventually developed into the highly organised banking industry, that has increasingly and wrongfully enslaved mankind in today's world.

Bankers are essentially money farmers who grow money by proxy, e.g. they loan seed-money to workers who can show that, by harvest time, the seeds will yield a handsome profit, which will enable them to give back the seed-money plus interest to the banker. Trading in money has long been the most desirable business of those who know the ultimate and true value of work and money. This gives them invisible power to control global financial affairs. Money has become the medium around which all life on earth revolves. Shekel philosophy has shackled mankind in slavery.

Money in the twenty first century is the vast invisible barrier surrounding the habitat of the majority of workers who are financially hamstrung. Though workers generate mountains of cash, most working couples cannot afford to buy a home unless they bind themselves to a mortgage that enslaves both husband and wife, forcing both of them to work for an average of thirty years, to free them from the bondage of borrowed money. Working routines of mortgage holders is so intense, that they are considered to be docile and easy to control, as they have little time for protesting and suchlike. Money is used to punish people who are found guilty in the courts. The police issue on the spot fines. Everyone must find money to buy food, medicine, entertainment, services and governments levy many kinds of questionable monetary taxes on their citizens. Powerful governments impose economic sanctions, commercial and financial penalties on targeted self-governing states, groups, or individuals. Economic sanctions may include various forms of trade barriers, tariffs, and restrictions on financial transactions.

Christians at all levels have naively and remarkably failed to recognize the consubstantial spiritual power in prayer, work, love, and money, and unsuspectingly trusted dishonest governments and bankers, to protect the fruit of their labour and use it to promote the common good

The phrase, "Love of money is the root of all evil" is well-known, however a more accurate definition is: "Love of money for personal satisfice is the root of all evil". Money is a sacred because it is the product of human brain and brawn, therefore money is not an evil thing, but evil people use it for evil purposes just like any other item at their disposal, e.g. stones are used to build comfortable homes and also used to stone people to death. The lifesaving hypodermic needle is also the executioner's tool and so on. Work is a sacred human activity but it too, is frequently used to do evil things. It is a fact that the power of money is being used for evil purposes is visible everywhere, especially, in the third world, where hungry people are forced to eat un-healthy food and to drink contaminated water, in the production of pornography, in the production of energy that pollutes the environment, in the production of personal weapons and weapons of mass destruction and to train military personnel how to use such weapons effectively, all done in order to accumulate even more money. War is the main market for the weapons industry and evil people initiate wars to increase sales of their military products. Money being the sacred fruit of sacred work should only be used to create and maintain a world of peace and plenty, it should never be used for evil purposes.

Jesus did not describe money as an evil thing, in fact He confirmed its sanctity, when He encouraged His followers to give this fruit of their labour to God to spread the 'Good News' and to create a world of love, peace and plenty. When the Pharisees questioned Jesus as to how the people should use their money, **He said, "Give to Caesar what is Caesar's and to God what is God's".** He thereby effectively instructed His followers to use some of their money to support legal governments that work for the common good and secondly, to do God's work, which includes the maintenance of one's own family, the needy and the church. God's money is the discretionary portion of a person's income, which is the portion that remains following the payment of all the essential household bills etc. It has been suggested that at least 10% of discretionary income and/or 10% of one's free time should be given to God. However, most people habitually and unconsciously dispose of God's money on consumer commodities to sate commercially induced appetites, while allowing greedy bankers to cream off unjustified portions of the worker's deposits passing through financial systems. The bankers do not use this money to support this hungry world which they have un-lovingly created by greed and neglect.

Jesus continually emphasised that love is the essential element that, enables humanity to develop and maintain a good relationship with God and neighbours.

"Beloved, let us love one another, for love is of
God; and everyone who loves is born of God
and knows God. He who does not love does
not know God, for God is love". (1 John 4:7)

How to love God? If one agrees and accepts God's divine
manifesto and is aware of the constancy of His love and His
bounty to sustain the lives of all living things, one is likely
to admire and **love** Him in return and live according to
His teaching.

How to love your neighbour? In the final analysis of
love, it is the one and only thing, one human can give
to another in the name of Jesus. An act of **love** is to freely
give one's self, either by word, restraint, deed or in goods.

Love by word. Is to perpetually forgive those who repent,
the giving one's time, listening, giving good advice,
expressing sympathy, imparting knowledge, conversing,
never tell lies and neither verbally or written injure another
person's good character.

Love by restraint. Is to be nonviolent in all circumstances
refusing to provide dangerous substances or instruments,
refusing to encourage someone to go to a dangerous place etc:

Love by deed, is physical **work** done in a multitude of
manual and mental disciplines, to improve the living
conditions of humanity and for the wellbeing of the
environment.

Love, is God's ultimate gift to mankind. When love is freely given, it is lovingly returned to the giver.

If no work is done, no love is gained and therefore it is very obvious that there is a direct connection, between **love** and **work** and it may be said that, **work is love.**

It is of the utmost importance that everyone should recognise the intrinsic value and dignity of **work** done in every human capacity, from the simplest to the most complicated task.

The un-Godly practices of the financial institutions have distorted Christian love by abusing the fruits of Christian labour, when they invest money generated by Christian workers to finance un-Christian projects, usually with false promises of vast monetary returns from such investments.

Money is the sacred element that contains the elixir of Jesus Christ
Love is the fruit of prayer
Work is the fruit of love
Money is the fruit of work
God's work is the fruit of Money
Miracles are the fruits of God's work
God's people use money to do God's work
Evil people use it to do Satan's work

MONASTICISM

The ultimate Christian vocation is to guard the financial affairs of Jesus Christ. There is an urgent need for new laicized monastic communities, with a brief, to study world economics in order to ensure, that the fruits of God's workers, are used in the best possible way, to fulfil Jesus Christ's Manifesto according to the Gospels and to show Christians how to eliminate 'Third World' poverty. They might adopt Saint Matthew as their patron, (he was originally a tax collector for the Romans) and use his name to identify their communities. They may adopt the ancient double monastic rule, where married and single people lived and worked together in open communities. They would aspire to be self- sufficient by growing fruit and vegetables and keeping poultry while pooling resources and salaries from outside 'day jobs' until they finally establish a community that is financial independent. This new order could eventually provide ethical banking services. They could organise barter groups and encourage individuals to practice cashless dealing and develop broad net-working to reduce expenses. They would preach that the combination of '**prayer, love, work and money**' is the sacred and visible manifestation of Jesus Christ administrating to the human race. They would encourage basic Christian families to adopt and practice monastic self-sufficiency and sharing, as the sacred way of living on essentials.

In the parable of the Good Samaritan Jesus taught His followers the divine value of love, work and money. Love mentally assesses a need and work fulfils that need.

The Samaritan went to the victim and bandaged his wounds, applying oil and wine. Then he used his donkey to carry the victim to an inn and took care of him. The next day he took out two denarii and gave them to the innkeeper. 'Look after him,' he said, 'and when I return, I will reimburse you for any extra expense you may have''. If the Good Samaritan had not dismounted his donkey and rolled up his sleeves and set to **work**, the unfortunate victim may have died in the ditch.

"Money and possessions are the second most referenced topic in the Bible. Money is mentioned more than 800 times and the message is clear: Nowhere in Scripture is debt viewed in a positive way. Jesus dwelt on misuse of money and its consequent ability to distort and destroy a person's relationship with God.

"In the same way, anyone of you who does not renounce all his possessions cannot be my disciple." Luke, 14:33

Blessed are the poor in spirit

The poor in spirit are those who believe that they are primarily servants of God and any talents, wealth or property that they possess was given to them by God.

They are God's willing stewards, exclusively using such wealth, talents and possessions to fulfil the teachings of Jesus Christ.

Money in the hands of evil people is the greatest weapon ever known. They use money to produce military hardware to make war and they use it to propagate programmes that encourage violence, discordancy, degradation and they have a history of disrespect for religion and native cultures.

In the hands of Jesus' people, money progresses the well-being of the human race. It is used to improve worldwide living conditions: such as medical, education food production, shelter/housing, clean water, infrastructure and much more and they also support those who preach love and nonviolence according to Jesus Christ's manifesto.

Catechism of the Catholic Church

Paragraph 901: 'Hence the laity, dedicated as they are to Christ and anointed by the Holy Spirit, are marvellously called and prepared so that even richer fruits of the Spirit may be produced in them. For all their works, prayers and apostolic undertakings, family and married life, daily work, relaxation of mind and body, if they are accomplished in the Spirit – indeed even the hardships of life if patiently born – all these become spiritual sacrifices acceptable to God through Jesus Christ. In the celebration of the Eucharist these may most fittingly be offered to the Father along with the body of the Lord. And so, worshipping everywhere by their holy actions, the laity [should] consecrate the world itself to God, everywhere offering worship by the holiness of their lives'.

Catholic priests have neglected to expand and expound the theology contained paragraph 901of the Catechism of the Catholic Church.

Jesus said in John 4:19, "Whoever loves God must also love his brother", in Luke 6:31 and Matt 7:12, "Do unto others as you would have them do unto you". Most of Jesus' parables deal with human relationships and human needs. All of which indicates, that He expects people to care for the needs of family and neighbours and they should never do anything to harm humanity or the environment, either directly or indirectly. Salvation is thereby achieved by people who learn to love God by loving and working to care for humanity and all creation. Everyone needs to be comfortable and totally conscious in the knowledge that God is monitoring their every thought and deed, such as people in supermarkets and other public places when they are doing what is correct, they are not perturbed knowing that they are being monitored by surveillance cameras.

During his three years of public life Jesus had much to say about work and money. Many of his parables dealt with work roles and commercial activities, which were practiced at that time. The socio-economic scale at that time (1% rich-99% poor) was not very different from today.

Jesus used parables to demonstrate how best to work and use money to do the work of God, attending to the needs of the poor, the sick, the oppressed, the prisoners, the environment and each other. Christians are encouraged to believe that protecting the environment is an obvious element of Jesus' message. The environment is where people live together with neighbours, flora and fauna. It is the water they drink and the air they breathe, it is where they build homes, it is where animals live and plants grow for all to eat. It is important to meditate on the fact, that every living thing must eat other living things whether, animal or vegetable or both in order to survive. People cannot care for themselves or their neighbours unless they take care of the environment. Jesus does not want them to destroy the earth with an over dependence on cars and other consumer items which pollute air and water and poison the soil. Mark 16:15. Jesus tells the Disciples to, "Go into all, the world and preach the Gospel to all **creation**". Rev; 21:1 "In Christ's future Kingdom the rest of **creation** will be transformed into a new Earth".

Jesus said, "You have heard that it hath been said. An eye for an eye, and a tooth for a tooth, but I say unto you, that you resist not evil but whosoever shall smite you on your right cheek, turn to him

the other also. If any man will sue you at the law, and take your coat, let him have your cloak also. Whosoever shall compel you to go a mile, go with him two, Give to him that asks you, and don't turn away from him that would borrow from you. You have heard that it has been said, you shall love your neighbour and hate your enemy, but I say to you, love your enemies, bless them that curse you, do good to them that hate you, and pray for them who despitefully use you and persecute you. Matt 5:38-44

Jesus also taught His followers to love one another, which in practice means to care and to support everyone. **Jesus said, "The poor you will always have among you". John 12:8.** The truly poor people are those who cannot support themselves, 1) People who were born with defects, physical or mental or both. 2) People who have had accidents and are disabled. 3) Those in prison have lost their independence and some are poor because they have given everything they had to the poor. Incurable sick people will always be poor. Jesus Christ does not expect His followers to allow greedy people to steal their money or their work and use it for immoral purposes or to bring suffering to others.

Workers can feed the hungry, give drink to the thirsty, clothe the naked, shelter the homeless, cure the sick, help prisoners and bury the dead and halt the unregulated destructive exploitation of Planet Earth if they were to use the power of the purse and adopt the simple but radical manifesto of Jesus Christ. Mark 12:17. "Give to Caesar what belongs to Caesar and to God what belongs to God". Giving at least10% of your discretionary income or at least 10% of your spare time to God, would solve 3rd world problems and make you a credible Christian.

The Holy Grail is the Consubstantial Power of: Prayer, Love, Work, and Money'

A suggestive theory that the sacred blood of Jesus Christ, which He shed as He was dying on the cross, was saved in a chalice called the Holy Grail. The search for the so-called miraculous receptacle containing His blood, 'the elixir of life', has long been a dream like obsession in some human minds. The sought after container is alleged to be the actual chalice Jesus used at His Last Supper. This legend has gained a measure of plausibility, in that, His Last Supper and His sacrificial Crucifixion together form the nucleus of Christianity, which is indeed the absolute elixir of life. Such notions of a 'Holy Grail' may have developed from the Holy Eucharist which Jesus instituted during His Last Supper. The Holy Eucharist contains the spiritual genetics of Christendom. One very important gene is the gene of love, which is the elixir Jesus gives to His followers. This is the elixir of the consubstantial power of **'prayer, work, love, and money'**. Prayer motivates love which motivates a person to work voluntarily, or by working to earn money to support and finance the common good. For example, person 'a' can support 'b' in person, or by proxy, if he or she, works to earn money to pay a person 'c' to support person 'b' who may be living locally or in a distant place. Assuming that a follower of Jesus has no wealth or property, the only thing he or she has to offer in sacrifice, is love in the form of voluntary work or in the form of money earned from work. Actual work or money, freely given for the well-being of others, is the greatest sacrifice a human being can offer to God short of martyrdom.

The work of human brain and brawn is conspicuously visible in every developed country throughout the world and it is sad that there is little or no recognisable spiritual recognition attached, to most of this human activity today.

An adamant characteristic in the teaching of Jesus is His insistence on the necessity of self-sacrifice. Again and again he goes back to the same thought, that men and women must lose their lives to gain their spiritual lives; that no one can be His disciple, unless they deny themselves and takes up their crosses and follow him.

"All the believers devoted themselves to the apostles' teaching, and to fellowship, and to sharing in meals (celebrating the Lord's Supper), and to prayer. A deep sense of awe came over them all, and the apostles performed many miraculous signs and wonders. And all the believers met together in one place and shared everything they had. They sold their property and possessions and shared the money with those in need. They worshiped together at the Temple each day, met in homes for the Lord's Supper, and shared their meals with great joy and generosity—all the while praising God and enjoying the goodwill of all the people. And each day the Lord added to their fellowship those who were being saved". Acts of the Apostles 2:42-4

Pope Francis said. "This is not communism, but pure Christianity".

Here we have a Christian community that is adhering to the teachings of Jesus Christ. They have developed a monastic way of living. It is noticeable that **they shared their money with those in need** in doing so they must have accepted the spirituality of money and did not see it as an evil thing. It is somewhat tragic that a spiritual aversion to money developed in the Catholic Church, in view of the fact that money has always been the means of supporting so much of the Church's work.

Priests find it very difficult to preach about the proper relationship, followers of Jesus Christ should cultivate with money. There is little prospect of the laity openly discussing their salaries, jobs, and shopping preferences regarding their Christian duty to practice the 'corporal works of mercy', this is because of ingrained perceptions that money is the key to personal comforts, health, success and admiration in the community. Money in their minds is generally considered to be a private matter, a matter, both wealthy and impoverished Christians would prefer to keep secret and avoid scrutiny. Individualism is a culture that is fostered by market capitalism which does not help the situation. People are left to make their own decisions regarding financial matters, in the hope that they will in good conscious adhere to God's will and generously contribute to the common good and support the needy.

The Church has been hampered because it has not theologically recognised the spirituality of money, thereby giving the impression that, it is not fully aware of the divine and supernatural power, which emanates from the conjoined energy of prayer, love, and the work of human hands that generates money.

The Catholic Church's reticence, to theologically recognise the consubstantial sanctity of **'prayer, work, love and money'**, as intrinsic ingredients from the teachings of Jesus Christ, has prevented it from achieving its full potential to evangelise the entire human family and improve the well-being of all, rather it has caused division, e.g. Martin Luther and the beginning of Protestantism which fragmented God's people.

Martin Luther was born on 10 November 1483 in Eisleben. His father was a copper miner. Luther studied at the University of Erfurt and in 1505 decided to join a monastic order, becoming an Augustinian friar. He was ordained in 1507and began teaching at the University of Wittenberg and in 1512 he was made a doctor of Theology. In 1510 he visited Rome on behalf of a number of Augustinian monasteries, and was appalled by the corruption he found there.

Luther became increasingly angry about the clergy selling 'indulgences' which promised remissions from God's punishments for the sins of the living and for those who had died and were possibly incarcerated in purgatory. On 31 October 1517, he published his '95 Theses', attacking papal abuses and the sale of indulgences.

The sale of indulgences is still a major economic source of finance in Catholicism. Perhaps it would be more in keeping with the teaching of Jesus and economically beneficial, if the hierarchy preached that Jesus has already indicated that the spiritual way to finance God's work is in St Mark's Gospel 12:17. The laity's donations to God by way of money and voluntary labour are real sacrifices that should be spiritually recognised and given a prominent part in the Holy Sacrifice of Mass and in the Eucharistic rituals of all Christian sects.

Martin Luther wrote, "The Apostle commands us to work with our hands so that we may give to the needy.... This is what makes caring for [one's own] body a Christian work, that through its health and comfort we may be able to work, to acquire, and lay by funds with which to aid those who are in need, that in this way the strong member may serve the weaker.... This is a truly Christian life".

It is essential to believe that to gain salvation it is necessary to make the supreme sacrifice, of giving a generous portion of one's work and of one's money earned from honest work, to God for the benefit of humanity.

Should this become a common Christian practice, it has the ecumenical potential to unify Christianity and eliminate world hunger by harnessing the financial energy of the entire Christian community.

An estimated 820 million people did not have enough to eat in 2018, up from 811 million in the previous year, which is the third year of increase in a row. This underscores the immense challenge of achieving the Sustainable Development Goal of Zero Hunger by 2030, says the new edition of the annual, '**The State of Food Security and Nutrition in the World',** This report was released in July 2019.

God's Money, is the fruit of human's ethically work and is therefore a sacred commodity. A doctrine defining the sanctity of money would elevate Jesus Christ, to a higher spiritual level in the minds of those who are working to establish a spiritual method for sharing God's bounty throughout mankind.

If all Christians were to adopt the simple Jesus Christ inspired theology of money, based on the power of prayer, love, work and the consequential spirituality of money, they could together establish a global spiritual philosophy of education and guidance, for all who are concerned for the wellbeing of mankind.

MONEY IS AN INSTRUMENT OF DISTRIBUTION

Why do Douglas Social Crediters always speak about money, the monetary system and the reform of the money system? Almost all the problems that concern us each day are money problems including not only the problems of individuals but also the problems of institutions, schools, universities and all levels of government. In today's world, one cannot live very long or very well without securing goods made by others. We cannot obtain others' products without paying for them with money. Even people not attached to money are obliged to have some if they don't want to end up in an early grave. Money is essentially a license to live. Not because we eat money nor wear money but because, without it, a person is limited to what they can personally produce. Some will call money an invention of the devil and a source of disorder, an instrument of domination and even a tool of perdition. Indeed it is the improper role and use of money and the flawed management of the money system that is diabolical and causes many despicable conditions. But money, as an instrument for the acquisition of goods and services, is an elegant social invention. Note that money is a sound mechanism for the disbursement of goods and services because it is precisely for consumption that an economy exists. Money easily facilitates consumption. Thanks to the existence of money, the farmer who has more potatoes than he needs for his family, and would like shoes for his children, is not obliged to find a shoemaker who has too many shoes and not enough potatoes. The same thing for the shoemaker: he is not obliged to go to the countryside to find a man who has too many potatoes but is without shoes. Both the farmer and shoemaker offer in the marketplace their surplus production. Using the portable tool for exchange called money, each can choose what they need from the array of available goods. Money offers flexibility but is not a commodity in itself. It can purchase either butter or a musical instrument, is universally accepted and can be exchanged by anyone for anything. Money is an instrument of distribution In itself, money is not much. A simple printed piece of paper with the number 5 on it allows me to buy $5 worth of goods. Another piece of paper, depicting the number 10, but not twice as large, twice as thick or twice as expensive to produce, allows me to purchase $10 worth of goods. One cannot distribute products that do not exist even if money were abundantly available. It would be absurd to say that we could survive with printed pieces of paper representing values if there were no goods. Distribute as much money as you like to someone who lives alone in the North Pole or in the desert! However, it is just as ridiculous to be without pieces of paper representing different values to exchange for products that are both available and essential for life. We should expect a just relationship between the products marked with a certain value, and the purchasing power, in the form of the right amount of money, in the hands of those who need those products. Is it bookkeeping? Exactly! On one side, there are products with prices. On the other side, there is purchasing power in the form of paper bills, coins made from metal and bank accounts consisting of numbers. With the equal sign between products and purchasing power, goods can pass with ease from the producer or retailer to the consumer who needs them. So, is our money system good? It would be a good system if the bookkeeping was accurate and if the numbers that allowed one to access goods were well distributed to each person. However, the masters of the system have spoiled it by invalid bookkeeping and an unfair distribution of numbers. The money masters are neither producers nor governments representing society. The numbers originate in banks and represent the profit wrested by the banking system. Presently, the volume of money has no relationship with a nation's production or productive capacity. Instead of being a simple bookkeeping system, the money system is a monopoly that operates as a tool of domination over our daily lives. The farmer may increase his production but the banker in charge of the money system does not correspondingly increase the amount of money in the system to allow for the purchase of the increased products available for sale at the farm gate. Numbers are more abundant when one produces guns and bombs, even though no thinking person wants this. Additional money is disbursed to wage-earners in the war business, even though their products have added nothing life-sustaining to anyone. This type of productivity only serves to increase prices and reduces the purchasing power of the volume of money in the system. We saw our great statesmen in all the civilized nations allow people to suffer for ten years during the Great Depression. Essential goods were not purchased for lack of money in the hands of the hungry populations. This was criminal. The false accountants, the bankers, acted criminally. Governments, elected to ensure the common good, were the accomplices of the criminals, whether from complicity, cowardice or foolishness. Do Douglas Social Crediters want to get rid of the whole system? Not at all. We consider money to be a matter of bookkeeping, but it must be a just system and in its present form it is anything but just. Money's proper role is to ensure a distribution of goods necessary to sustain life. Since money is a claim on goods and services the population must have enough of it to obtain what they need as quickly as the system can produce. Each person must have a sufficient share of this power to purchase as each of us has a right to live; this right requires money. That is what Douglas Social Credit proposes: 1 The establishment of a Credit Office that would keep a record of total production and consumption (destruction or depreciation) in the country or province. 1 A total volume of purchasing power correlated to the productive capacity of the nation or province. The volume must be justly distributed to each member of the nation, through: 1 Payment for work, disbursed by employers; 1 A periodic Dividend issued to each person, regardless of employment status, from birth to death. The Dividend would be issued by the Credit Office; 1 A reduction of prices, compensated to the retailer by the Credit Office. The Compensated Discount would banish inflation. Where would the Credit Office get the money for the Dividend and the Compensated Discount? Since money is simply numbers used to obtain things based on a nation's productivity, the Credit Office would simply issue the right volume of numbers. It is only a matter of bookkeeping. Technical matters will not be detailed here as there are a variety of methods from which to choose. (One method is discussed in the booklet by Louis Even, A Sound and Efficient Financial System.) Essentially, a Dividend can be entered as a credit in an account opened for the personal use of each citizen. A similar credit can be issued to a retailer on the presentation of discount vouchers. Do you think these credits would circulate and be accepted like money? Certainly! Credits circulate and are accepted today. Loans and overdrafts are only figures for the use of manufacturers, retailers and citizens. Such credits allowed leaders such as Mackenzie King, Roosevelt and Churchill to conduct six years of human slaughter during the Second World War. The credits were not gold, silver nor even paper, but mere figures entered into accounts and mobilized through cheques. Do you think a money system can be run just like that? It is preferred that a just money system be run by society rather than allow money to control society. There is nothing arbitrary in the monetary bookkeeping proposed by Clifford Hugh Douglas' system. Production remains the business of the producers and consumption remains the business of consumers. Accountants at the Credit Office would record both totals, and calculate and balance what is lacking on one side and make it equal to the other. There would be no expropriation, no nationalization and no decrees dictating what should be produced or consumed. We would have a perfect system of economic democracy with Douglas Social Credit. Everything should remain the business of free persons. Freedom would be maximized as sufficient purchasing power allowed citizens to obtain products of their choosing. This is superior to the limited options of citizens who have empty wallets. Louis Even.

MICHAEL JOURNAL May/June/July 2021.
THE ULTIMATE REVOLUTION

All the manufactured items in the world have been fashioned from animal, mineral, or vegetable raw materials or a combination thereof. These raw materials have been present on earth since the dawn of time. Man and animal has been aware of the importance of raw materials from the very beginning, since possession of food producing territory has traditionally ensured the survival of the community and the species. The urge to protect the one's food producing territory has long been a matter of instinct. This territorial instinct is a 'basic instinct' and it is no wonder that so many of our wars have been conflicts concerning territory, and it has always been easy for the military men to enlist recruits by appealing to their territorial instincts, with propaganda of invaders confiscating land, homes and violating women.

All raw materials are obtained from rock, soil, water, atmosphere, forests, fauna and sunlight these are the common birthrights of all mankind. An individual who claims personal ownership of any of these materials is a thief violating the commandment, "You shall not steal". Many thousands of years of human progression has developed a democratic system, designed to ensure that a fair share of the Earth's resources should be available to the entire global family. Democracy dictates that, it is no longer necessary for any individual, to stand guard over his food producing piece of earth, because the democratic process ensures, that his food will always be available to him, while he works to produce goods from raw materials in another parts of the system. It is basically a modernised version of the age old barter system, when labour and food was exchanged directly for labour and food. People now exchange their labour for an agreed sum of money, which in turn allows them to purchase food and goods manufactured by others. Money has become the blood flowing in the earth's commercial veins, and financial institutions regulate the monetary systems which are immorally biased to enable rich people to acquire more and more wealth, that is frequently used for immoral and evil purposes.

The global financial system works well, in that it enables everyone to move money here and there and everywhere easily and quickly. Unfortunately, money moves away from developing countries too quickly and is very slow to return to such places. A lack of money in developing countries has created conditions, which dictate, that half of the global community is currently poor, starving, disease prone and chronically under-educated. People continually make voluntary contributions from their wages, to support worthy projects but such funds have had little impact on the over-all situation in the Third World, and many people believe that a final solution can only come from governments and financial institutions, in spite of historical knowledge, that these have traditionally refused to provide sufficient resources to put everything in order. The financial institutions have shown a marked reluctance to make the necessary funds available to the Third World, preferring always to invest their money in projects, which accumulate more money, often in schemes, which are directly detrimental to poor countries. Images of famine and degradation in many parts of the world have scandalised ordinary people for a long time, and many are asking in desperation, 'what, can we do?' 'Is there no end to this nightmare?' 'Why are we so helpless'?

The solution is simple but radical. The 'Meek' must continue to do what they do best, i.e. the creation of wealth, but they must accept, that they have a 'moral' responsibility to ensure, that the wealth which they create is used for the common good. The time has come for the Meek to assert their power and their authority. They must conceive a new institution and be prepared for intense pains at its birth. They must inherit the Earth as forecast by Jesus.

Who are the Meek? The Meek have been described by various civilisations in different ways; slaves, the proletariat; the salaried collectively; the uncultured; the lowest class of citizens; etc.: However, they are by far the most numerous members of the human family and they are the primary creators of wealth. They provide services, grow crops, make machines and manufacture goods and foods from animal, vegetable and mineral raw materials, which are initially obtained free of charge from the earth, but with the input of human labour, these materials increase in value in proportion to the amount of labour invested in each article, e.g.; the basic value of house is calculated by the quantity of direct and indirect labour involved in its construction, and gold, like all the other minerals has been present on earth since the our World was formed, but the huge expenditure of labour in finding it, makes precious metals very expensive.

The Meek can inherit the earth by taking control of the wealth which they produce, ensuring such wealth can never be weaponized. The time has come for the Meek to adopt a new philosophy, which states, **'Those who create wealth have a duty and a responsibility to ensure that such wealth, is used for the Common Good'**. This philosophy is justified by the fact that all wealth is derived from God given raw material, which is the birth-right of the entire human family. The Meek have traditionally allowed the commercial sector, and the financial institutions to retain a portion of newly created wealth, on the understanding that they use it for the benefit of all, but it has become very clear that greedy people, have been diverting the bulk of such wealth into private pockets, bringing starvation and degradation to half of mankind in the process. This practice has created a seething mass of hungry, vulnerable people often wounded and traumatised by weapons that were made from the money which the Meek produced. This practice has to stop.

How can the Meek control the distribution of the Wealth, which they create?

Jesus Christ has shown the way! He said; "Give to God what belongs to God" and He implied it was necessary to give to the Caesarean government what is needed to civilly provide and maintain all that has been agreed for the convenience of the community but what really belongs to God? Make no mistake, Jesus commanded His followers to work exclusively for God on a 24/7 basis, to achieve God's plan, for the wellbeing of all creation. It is reasonable to calculate that if all Christians were to give, at least10% of their discretionary income and at least10% of their spare time to God, that they could establish a Christ like communal unity and bona-fides for doing God's work, i.e., educating the masses, feeding the hungry, giving drink to the thirsty, clothing the naked, sheltering the homeless, visiting the sick, visiting prisoners and burying the dead and etc.

Regular donations of money and/or voluntary work to help the needy, brings authority and creditability to those who make such sacrifices. By responding positively to God's command to give Him the money and the work that belongs to Him, the Meek will gain the creditability of love, giving them the confidence to approach every commercial company, supermarket, financial institution, with whom they have dealings, and appeal to them to contribute at least 10% from the discretionary portion of their net profit to help the needy. In fact some companies are already contributing to charities from their profits; e.g., computers for schools etc. The Meek collectively have unlimited and untested boycotting muscle in this area. **Genteel, concerted and polite refusals** by tens of millions of ordinary people, to cooperate with business owners and directors of financial institutions, who refuse to give 10% of their discretionary profit, will ultimately be compelled, to respond positively to God's command and agree to contribute to this scheme.

Simple non-violent action of the Meek could ensure that at least 10% of the discretionary portion of the world's wealth is used, for the elimination of poverty at home and abroad, for education, medical services, etc: The commercial world would carry on as normal but they would have less cash to speculate with than at present. The cash generated by this scheme would create a new world economy, with a series of new and exciting industries specially orientated towards a peaceful world bringing security of food supplies, medicine, education, work, happiness and friendship to people everywhere.

The objectives of the Meek can only be achieved if the entire Christian community accept that, this proposal complies with Jesus Christ's metaphor in His parable of the Good Samaritan, which instructs His followers to attend to the needs of all those who are wounded and distressed. Christian families could adopt a spiritual monastic life style of living on essentials without the influence of consumer ethics, in the clear knowledge that they are spiritual monastic cells, generating their own discretionary income to finance necessary services such as industrial food production and establish a range of other badly needed facilities.

Christians will experience personal pain of conscience when calculating their discretionary income. There will be a dangerous backlash from those opposed to this programme and many of the Meek will be persecuted and marginalized or worse. Corrupt temptations to abuse the power of money is well known but the Meek will learn to deal with possible infringements within their organisation. There will be scandals among the Meek and false accusations at every turn but the Meek know that they will be successful because Jesus said "The Meek will inherit the Earth", so don't be afraid, give your 10% and support companies that agree to contribute at least 10% of their discretionary net profits, and do not support the companies who refuse. If you have money to invest, place it with ethical and environmentally friendly developments. Do not apply for employment in companies that disadvantage people or damage the environment. Do not waste personal energy protesting in the streets and do not become involved in violence or the destruction of property. Use your entire being to persuade those you know, to join this scheme to change the world. Use your ingenuity to research and develop methods and systems to improve the health and happiness of the human race. Protect the environment while you research ways and means of making all the world's resources available to everyone. Research the root cause of poverty in all its forms and find ways to prevent it and ultimately to eliminate it. Support research into the causes of disease and promote the production of affordable medicines for all. The Meek already have the necessary skills to tackle the foregoing but they do not have the funds or the organization to achieve the objectives outlined above. The greatest challenge for the Meek is to find ways, to motivate the masses of the world to become involved in this peaceful movement, and to harness the energy of every individual for the benefit of the entire human family. **"Hearts are streams – if they meet they become Rivers"**.

It has to start at grass root level and remain a grass root movement without boundaries. The Meek could form themselves into local groups of manageable proportions, and anybody who agrees to contribute at least 10% of his or her's discretionary income, and/or at least 10% of discretionary spare time to do God's work is eligible for membership. Money collected should be temporally lodged in financial institutions that agree to contribute at least 10% of their discretionary net profits, if no such institution exists, use the friendliest banks available until you establish your own permanent financial body to manage and keep accounts of God's money.

As the Meek communities grow, so will their financial strength increase and each local group will collectively decide how best to use the accumulating funds, some will be needed locally and the remainder could be transferred to a central fund to finance the development of new industries and schemes to support the poor. Each local group appoints two members to a Regional Group, each Regional Group appoints two members to a National Group each National Group appoints two members to an International Group. The National Group should organize and supervise the collection of monies donated by participating industrial companies. The International Group would liaise with National Groups who would liaise with recognised charitable bodies that work for God in their own countries. Modern technology should be embraced to organise and manage the community's affairs. This is a simple blueprint for a non- violent revolution, based on the teachings of Jesus Christ. His followers have the potential power to change civilization, and to make the world a spiritual place of plenty, peace and happiness, if they work exclusively for God by using the power of their work and money. Jesus Christ's wish for unity among all Christian communities is possible if only they would spiritually work together and harness the consequential energy generated by their work and money, for global common good and counter current liberal laicized, subtle, concerted and insidiously promoted opposition to Jesus Christ.

Sam Walton, the founder of Walmart left a very relevant metaphor regarding the power of money when he said; "There is only one boss; the customer. And he can fire everybody in the company from the chairman on down, simply by spending his money somewhere else".

If all Christians were consciously aware of the great difference they could make, regarding the wellbeing of the needy, by simply choosing to purchase only the things they really need. People frequently complain about bad TV programmes, shoddy goods and inferior services, none of these would exist if people refused to buy them.

If Hierarchy of the Catholic Church were to allow The Holy Spirit to open their eyes, they might see the real Jesus Christ in the real world, they would soon learn that the necessary energy and wherewithal to power the spreading of His Good News around the whole world is clearly visible, and available in the entire human family, that is waiting for direction, guidance and spiritual support in doing God's work.

It is necessary that Christians should study the ungodly 'Money Moguls' methods of harvesting and misusing Christian worker's money. Christians should acquaint themselves with current financial systems with a view to setting up their own systems to cater for all who work for God. Christians would be very happy, if they knew for certain that their sacrifices of money and voluntary work, was spiritually recognised as sacred contributions to God's program, to bring peace and plenty to mankind.

APPENDIX 1: U.S. WAR STATISTICS

War	Date	Killed in Battle or Died of Wounds	Died of Disease, Accident, etc.	Total American Deaths	Legal Authority
World War II	1941-45	291,557	113,842	405,399	Formal declaration
Civil War (US+CS)	1861-65	204,070 [US:_110,070] [CS:_94,000]	414,152 [US:_250,152] [CS:_164,000]	618,222 [US:_360,222] [CS:_258,000]	USA:_Executive CSA:_ Revolutionary
World War I	1917-18	53,402	63,114	116,516	Formal declaration
Vietnam War	1965-73	47,378	10,799	58,177	Executive
Korean War	1950-53	33,741	2,827	36,568	Executive
Revolutionary War	1775-83	Patriot: 6,824 Loyalist: 1,700	Patriot: 18,500	Patriot: 25,324 Loyalist: 7,000	Patriot: Revolutionary Loyalist: Royal
Iraq War	2003- (as of Aug. 21, 2011)	3,480	928	4,408	Executive
Indian Wars	1775-1891	3,000 ±	1,100 ±	4,100 ±	Executive
War of 1812	1812-15	2,260	17,205	19,465	Formal declaration
Mexican War	1846-48	1,733	11,550	13,283	Formal declaration
Afghanistan	2001- (as of Aug. 21, 2011)	1,360	273	1,633	Executive
Philippine Insurgency	1899-1902	1,018	3,216	4,234	Executive

Spanish Civil War (Abraham Lincoln Battalion)	*1936-39*			*900*	*Volunteers*
Texas War of Independence	*1835-36*	*704*			*Revolutionary*
Spanish-American War	1898	385	2,061	2,446	Formal declaration
Nicaragua (Walker's Expedition)	*1856-57*			*1,000*	*Filibuster*
Russian Civil War	1918-20	304	268	572	Executive
Lebanon	1982–84	273		273	Executive
Gulf War	1990-91	148	235	383	Executive
Mexican expeditions	1914-17	67		67	Executive
War against Terrorism	2001–	66	82	148	Executive

APPENDIX 2: CRYPTIC MASONIC SYMBOLS

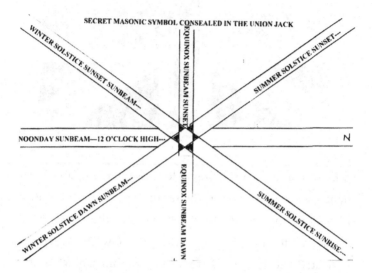

SECRET MASONIC SYMBOL CONSEALED IN THE UNION JACK

WINTER SOLSTICE SUNSET SUNBEAM—

EQUINOX SUNBEAM SUNSET

SUMMER SOLSTICE SUNSET—

NOONDAY SUNBEAM—12 O'CLOCK HIGH---

N

WINTER SOLSTICE DAWN SUNBEAM—

EQUINOX SUNBEAM DAWN

SUMMER SOLSTICE SUNRISE—

In 1707 Scottish and English Freemasons conjured up a secret Masonic treaty to amalgamate their two states, to increase Masonic control of Great Britain's monetary matters and to protect their own executive privileges. They considered it necessary to create a new national flag that would conceal their secret symbol while strongly appealing to Christian people, they published a 'cock and bull' spiel, to intertwine the English Cross of St George with the Scottish Cross of St Andrew (and later with the Irish Cross of St Patrick in 1801) to signify God's blessings on the unity of the three countries in the Union Jack. The Masonic media then promoted the Union in euphoria terms, to encourage the people of the so-called British Isles to worship a secret masonic monarchy, to endeavour through their work to make Britain Great and to defend the Union with their lives if duty called on them to do so, in glorious wars secretively initiated by Mason and their Zionist friends, where Christians mostly killed Christians. Freemasonry Field Marshall Douglas Haig ordered his soldiers to do their duty at the Battle of the Somme on 1ˢᵗ July 1916, wearing a steel helmet to protect the head and only uniforms to protect the body against deadly machine gun fire, (it was like the Zulus who went into battle almost naked in 1879). The heaviest loss of life for British Army occurred on that July day, 57,470 casualties (19240) fatal. Following the war he was nicknamed "Butcher Haig" for the two million British and Irish casualties killed or injured under his command.

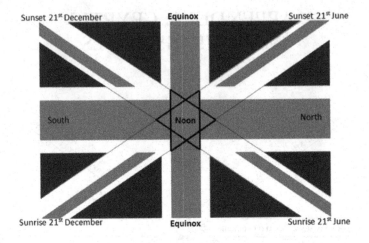

Sunset 21st December   Equinox   Sunset 21st June

South   Noon   North

Sunrise 21st December   Equinox   Sunrise 21st June

In Egyptian sun worshipping, Horus is the rising sun, RA is the noon sun and Osiris is the setting sun. Jews and Masons show great interest in the Sun Gods and the construction of massive temples and pyramids and how the Egyptians motivated the hordes of stone-masons and labourers. Dr. Zahi Hawass, believes the pyramid builders were motivated by higher forces. They were proud of their work, because they were not just building the tomb of a king. They were free men, building Egypt and everyone was a participant and worked out of reverence for the Sun God RA, the most important deity in Egyptian mythology who was the supreme power in the universe and the giver of life. Jews and Masons learned from the Egyptians, that in order to motivate the modern masses they needed to create an objective that spiritually appealed to workers and soldiers, to give them a higher reason to obey their masters.

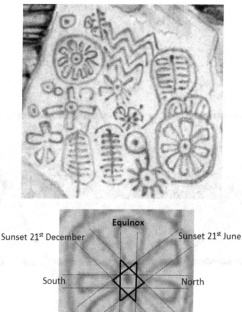

Equinox

Sunset 21ˢᵗ December

Sunset 21ˢᵗ June

South

North

Sunrise 21ˢᵗ December

Sunrise 21ˢᵗ June

Equinox

6,000 year old inscriptions from the stones at
Loughcrew Megalithic Centre
Boyne Valley, County Meath, Ireland

6,000 year old sun worshipping inscriptions

Loughcrew Megalithic Tumulus,
Boyne Valley Tours, County Meath, Ireland

This symbol shows the 'Fleur de Lis' imprisoned within the 'Star of David' indicating Zionist-Masonic influence in French affairs since 1789, the year of the French Revolution.

The French Revolution had given the Jews their first political victory and Napoleon personally gave them their second on the 22nd May 1799, when he published a proclamation inviting the Jews of Asia and Africa to submit to his flag, in order to re-establish ancient Jerusalem. Abbé Lemann said, "They grovelled in front of him and were ready to recognise him as their Messiah". "Blessed forever is the Lord, the God of Israel, Who has placed on the throne of France and the kingdom of Italy a prince according to His heart. God has seen the humiliation of the descendants of ancient Jacob and He has chosen Napoleon the Great to be the instrument of His mercy...Reunited today under his powerful protection in the good town of Paris, to the number of seventy-one doctors of the law and notables of Israel, we constitute a Great Sanhedrin, so as to find in us a means and power to create religious ordinances in conformity with the principles of our holy laws, and which may serve as a rule and example to all Israelites. These ordinances will teach the nations that our dogmas are consistent with the civil laws under which we live, and do not separate us at all from the society of men". The Masons have adopted the Jewish Star of David .

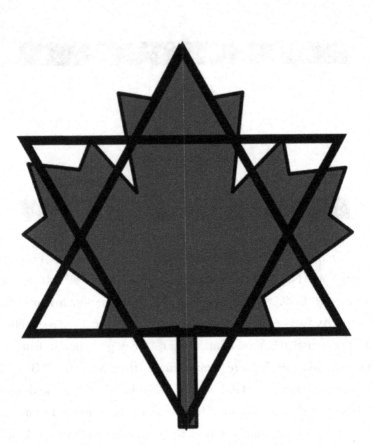

On February 15, 1965, after prolonged debate, a distinctively Canadian flag incorporating the sugar Maple leaf to form a double triangle representing the Zionist-Masonic association was adopted, to take the place of the so-called Red Ensign. The prime mover in this discussion was the Honorable John Ross Matheson, who had been initiated in Queen's Lodge, No 578, Kingston, in 1940.

FREEMASONRY OBELISKS CAN BE
SEEN ALL OVER THE WORLD

Some prominent in the USA are:-
The Washington Monument, Wall Street and Central Park
New York, San Antonio, Texas

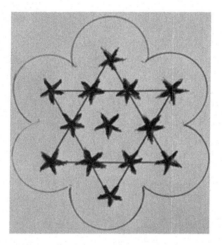

The Maple Sugar Leaf is the state symbol of:
New York, Rhode Island, Vermont, West Virginia
and Wisconsin
Clearly advertising Zionist-Masonic connections.

Printed in the United States
by Baker & Taylor Publisher Services